Windows Troubleshooting Series

Mike Halsey, MVP
Series Editor

Apress®

Windows
Networking
Troubleshooting

Mike Halsey
Joli Ballew

Apress®

Windows Networking Troubleshooting

Mike Halsey
Sheffield, South Yorkshire, UK

Joli Ballew
Garland, Texas, USA

ISBN-13 (pbk): 978-1-4842-3221-7
https://doi.org/10.1007/978-1-4842-3222-4

ISBN-13 (electronic): 978-1-4842-3222-4

Library of Congress Control Number: 2017958354

Managing Director: Welmoed Spahr
Editorial Director: Todd Green
Acquisitions Editor: Gwenan Spearing
Development Editor: Laura Berendson
Technical Reviewer: Massimo Nardone
Coordinating Editor: Nancy Chen
Copy Editor: Kim Wimpsett
Compositor: SPi Global
Indexer: SPi Global
Artist: eStudio Calamar

Distributed to the book trade worldwide by Springer Science+Business Media New York, 233 Spring Street, 6th Floor, New York, NY 10013. Phone 1-800-SPRINGER, fax (201) 348-4505, e-mail orders-ny@springer-sbm.com, or visit www.springeronline.com. Apress Media, LLC is a California LLC and the sole member (owner) is Springer Science + Business Media Finance Inc (SSBM Finance Inc). SSBM Finance Inc is a **Delaware** corporation.

For information on translations, please e-mail rights@apress.com, or visit www.apress.com/rights-permissions.

Apress titles may be purchased in bulk for academic, corporate, or promotional use. eBook versions and licenses are also available for most titles. For more information, reference our Print and eBook Bulk Sales web page at www.apress.com/bulk-sales.

Any source code or other supplementary material referenced by the author in this book is available to readers on GitHub via the book's product page, located at www.apress.com/9781484232217. For more detailed information, please visit www.apress.com/source-code.

Printed on acid-free paper

Contents at a Glance

Contents

About the Authors

Mike Halsey was first awarded as a Microsoft Most Valuable Professional (MVP) in 2011. He is the author of more than a dozen Windows books, including *Troubleshooting Windows 7: Inside Out, Troubleshoot and Optimize Windows 8: Inside Out, Windows 10 Troubleshooting*, and *The Windows 10 Accessibility Handbook* from Apress. He is also the author of other books in the Windows Troubleshooting Series. Based in Sheffield, United Kingdom, where he lives with his rescue border collies, Evan and Robbie, he gives many talks on Windows subjects from productivity to security, and he makes how-to and troubleshooting videos under the banner Windows.Do. You can follow him on Facebook and Twitter at @MikeHalsey.

Joli Ballew is a Microsoft MVP and Windows expert. She has written almost 60 books, most on Windows technologies. She currently works at Lynda.com authoring and filming training videos; is an adjunct professor of technology at Brookhaven College in Farmers Branch, Texas; and teaches Microsoft certification boot camps at Collin College in Plano, Texas. Joli spends her spare time doing yoga and running and enjoys being with her family.

About the Technical Reviewer

Massimo Nardone has more than 23 years of experience in security, web/mobile development, cloud computing, and IT architecture. His true IT passions are security and Android.

He currently works as the chief information security officer (CISO) for Cargotec Oyj and is a member of the ISACA Finland Chapter board. Over his long career, he has held these positions: project manager, software engineer, research engineer, chief security architect, information security manager, PCI/SCADA auditor, and senior lead IT security/cloud/SCADA architect. In addition, he has been a visiting lecturer and supervisor for exercises at the Networking Laboratory of the Helsinki University of Technology (Aalto University).

Massimo has a master of science degree in computing science from the University of Salerno in Italy, and he holds four international patents (PKI, SIP, SAML, and proxy areas). Besides working on this book, Massimo has reviewed more than 40 IT books for different publishing companies and is the coauthor of *Pro Android Games* (Apress, 2015).

Windows Troubleshooting Series

When something goes wrong with technology, it can seem impossible to diagnose and repair the problem, and harder still to prevent a recurrence. In this series of books, we'll take you inside the workings of your devices and software and teach you how to find and fix the problems using a simple step-by-step approach that helps you understand the cause, the solution, and the tools required.

Series Editor
Mike Halsey, MVP

As a Microsoft Most Valuable Professional (MVP) awardee since 2011, the author of more than a dozen books on Microsoft Windows, and a teacher for many years, Mike Halsey understands the need to convey complex subjects in clear and nonintimidating ways.

He believes that the Windows Troubleshooting Series is a great example of how quality help, support, and tutorials can be delivered to individuals of all technical ability. He hopes you enjoy reading this and many other books in this series, both now and for years to come.

CHAPTER 1

■ ■ ■

Understanding Networks

Despite the advent of the personal computer revolution in the late 1970s/early 1980s, computer networking can be traced all the way back to the early 1950s, more than 20 years earlier. Perhaps unsurprisingly, it's yet another technology that grew out of the Second World War, with one of the first implementations being the connection of U.S. military radar systems.

The advent of what has come to be known as the Internet can also be traced back before the Advanced Research Projects Agency Network (ARPANET) system in 1969 to an earlier project run by the creators of ARPANET, the Defense Advanced Research Projects Agency (DARPA), in 1962, just four years after the organization's creation. This is an organization that is still developing cutting-edge technologies today.

In fact, the networking of personal computer systems arrived comparatively late, with many businesses still using stand-alone IBM PCs, PC clones, and Apple computers until the widespread adoption of 10Base-type networks from companies such as Novell in the mid-1980s, which sometimes required a specially modified operating system to work. These were typically custom networking solutions operating over coaxial cable (the cable that was also used to connect your television to its antenna).

10Base-type networks could theoretically handle traffic up to 10Mbps, though in reality, cable limitations such as signal leakage and interference frequently dropped this to as little as 4Mbps.

Because coaxial cable is an analog, and not a digital, signal technology, configuration could often be tricky. Parameters such as baud rate (the signal modulation rate in pulses per second), initialization strings, and attention commands (AT) needed to be manually configured on each PC, and different networks would use different configurations.

These days we frequently take networking speeds of 100Gbps for granted (80,000 times faster than the maximum theoretical speed of the original 10Base networks). The digital Ethernet connections we use today were first developed in the 1970s by Xerox, Intel, and the Digital Equipment Corporation, and they helped bring about networking standards in 1983, which grew into the widespread adoption of digital networks after the advent of the Category 5 network cable, which we still use today.

Indeed, the networking we use to connect our PCs and devices to each other, and to the Internet, is still constantly evolving. We've been using Wi-Fi since the late 1990s, though it's gone through many changes and upgrades during this time and has gradually evolved to other networking standards, such as cellular and superfast wireless broadband networks.

© Mike Halsey and Joli Ballew 2017
M. Halsey and J. Ballew, *Windows Networking Troubleshooting*,
https://doi.org/10.1007/978-1-4842-3222-4_1

The pace of change of networking over the past 50 years has been so pronounced that, just as with other technologies such as displays, processors, and the Internet, it's difficult to accurately predict where it'll be 10 or 20 years from now. We're already seeing wireless connections for displays, and Bluetooth connections for peripherals are commonplace. All of these are networking technologies, and all grew from the work of DARPA in the 1960s.

Fortunately, or perhaps unfortunately depending on how you view these things, the standards for networking are well-established and rarely change, with each new technology ratified by the Institute of Electrical and Electronics Engineers (IEEE) before moving into widespread production. This may hold back our networking potential in years to come, as new standards and technologies will be inevitably required to leverage the full potential of what we'll be using in the future, and ratification can sometimes take time. For now, however, these standards help make networking straightforward and simple to configure and maintain.

My Network Is Bigger Than Your Network!

But, I hear you ask, how does this simplicity explain the fact that my company network is constantly suffering from outages, bottlenecks, and misconfigured devices?

The networking problems we face today are commonly linked to the complexity of the networks we create. If you look at a typical business, there will be tens, hundreds, thousands, or even tens of thousands of PCs connected to one or more servers, switches, and a router. There will also be other network devices in use, including Network Attached Storage (NAS) drives, networked printers, video-conferencing systems, security camera systems, and more besides. On top of this, the company will operate one or more Wi-Fi networks, and to each of these will be connected a PC, laptop, tablet, or smartphone running one of several different types of operating system, each with its own configuration options and remote management challenges. When you throw secure virtual private networks (VPNs) into the mix to allow the workforce to securely tunnel into the company network from home, other offices, or client and public locations over Wi-Fi or mobile broadband, you quickly come to realize just how complex the networks we take for granted today can be.

Expand this into the wider world, and we not only encounter the networks of other companies but those of vast datacenters, national wired and wireless telephony and data systems, and connections to satellites in orbit. All of this requires constant observation and management, so even a company with dedicated network management personnel, of which you may be one, won't be able to solve every problem that occurs. Everything is, quite literally, connected to everything else.

In reality, you're unlikely to be asked to repair a networking problem with a satellite in orbit (though if you are, please send us a photo). It's much more likely that the problem you face will be either local to a PC or single device or confined to a small area. Major outages tend to be easier to diagnose, such as a bulldozer at the construction site next door that has ripped through the main fiber-optic cabling outside, or one of your service providers is itself suffering an outage. So, what are the different types of network systems and hardware you're likely to use and encounter?

HOSTS, LMHOSTS, and WINS

You may never use it, but your Windows PC has a little file hidden away in the Windows directory called HOSTS, which you can find in the %windir%\system32\drivers\etc folder. In fact, all operating systems come with a version of this file, including Google's Android and Apple's iOS and OS X operating systems.

The HOSTS file, as shown in Figure 1-1, is used to map hostnames (local network, intranet, or domain names) to specific IP addresses online or on the local network (though perhaps it's most commonly used to point web sites such as Amazon and Facebook to the IP address 0.0.0.0 so as to make them inaccessible to the user because that address doesn't point to anything).

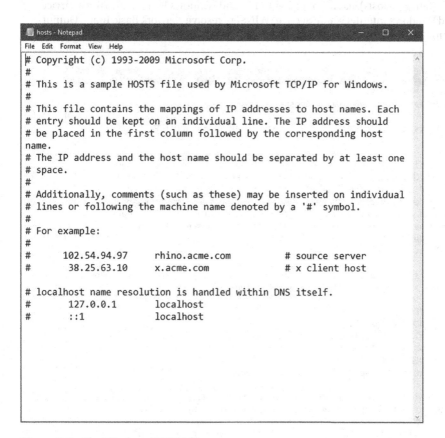

Figure 1-1. The Windows HOSTS file

The HOSTS file is not commonly used on modern PCs and computing devices, as the Domain Name System (DNS) takes care of name resolution (see the following note), which is the mapping of hostnames to IP addresses on the Internet and your local networks.

■ **Note** *Name resolution* is the process of retrieving the underlying numeric address values for computers and network resources, where the operating system has permitted easily remembered string names to be assigned as the identify of a computer, or resource, for use by the user. On Windows PCs, this refers to the process of retrieving the underlying IP address needed to communicate with a host or domain that is identified by a text-based computer name, or a domain address.

Windows PCs also come with a file in the same directory as HOSTS, called LMHOSTS (LAN Manager Hosts), as shown in Figure 1-2, and Windows PCs can also use a service called Windows Internet Name Service (WINS) to resolve Network Basic Input/Output System (NetBIOS) names to IP addresses.

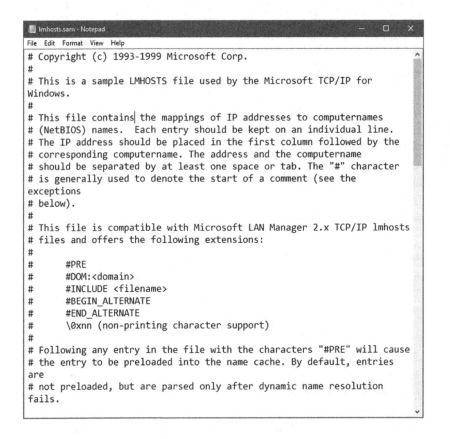

Figure 1-2. *The LMHOSTS file*

WINS was Microsoft's own alternative to DNS and is now used by only a few *very* old legacy applications and systems. You shouldn't be using WINS on your PCs unless you still have machines running Windows 95, Windows 98, or Windows Me on your network (and why would you want to do that?) as these systems will still need the NetBIOS system to find domain controllers and other computers on LAN networks. NetBIOS differs from the fully qualified domain names (FQDNs) that DNS and HOSTS use by allowing only 15-character computer names with no domain name component.

On modern PCs, FQDNs are used for this job instead, but if you think you may have NetBIOS devices on your network or applications on your PC, you can monitor your network for traffic on UDP port 137, which is the port that WINS uses for the NetBIOS service.

WINS exists in Windows today only to enable backward compatibility with older systems. Should you find that you do need to configure WINS, Microsoft has a technical reference online, which you can find at http://pcs.tv/2eRhWdn, and the LMHOSTS file contains instructions on how you can use it to create mappings of IP addresses to NetBIOS names.

Enterprise Networks

Network engineers create enterprise networks to serve large companies, corporations, and, well, enterprises. The main purpose of such a network is to securely connect workstations, domain controllers, various types of servers, devices, and numerous other resources, and to make those resources available to users based on their NTFS and Share permissions as well as their position in the company.

For example, network administrators will typically have full control over the physical network but likely won't have access to any specific employee data, such as Social Security numbers. And, while human resources employees will have access to employees' personal information, they likely won't have access to information regarding sales and inventory, and they certainly can't perform network tasks such as configuring a print server or installing a domain controller.

Of course, there are other reasons for having an enterprise network, including but not limited to managing data storage and configuring remote access, but what we want to offer right now is simply a general description of what an enterprise network offers so we can segue into our main topic, authentication technologies.

Authentication Technologies

To access an enterprise network and the resources on it, two things must happen. The user must supply credentials to authenticate who they are, and those credentials must be examined by an authentication server. If those credentials are valid, access to the network is granted. As part of this process, authorization to resources is also given, as applicable to that specific user.

Authorization defines what the user can and can't access while connected to the network and involves both Share and NTFS permissions, group membership, and more. Authentication and authorization are two vastly different areas of study. Here we're going to talk about authentication and how user credentials are protected during the login process.

In the most basic authentication scenario, a user sits at their assigned workstation, on-site, in the company's building. The user types their username and password, and those credentials are passed along the local network and authenticated by the designated authentication server. Even in this simple scenario, those credentials must be encrypted and secured. It would be a disaster if those credentials were somehow obtained by a hacker, perhaps one sitting outside the building with a sniffing device. In another scenario, the user is off-site, using a personal laptop, and accesses the company network over the Internet.

Whatever the case, protecting credentials and authentication must be a secure process. This is where authentication protocols come in. In computing, a protocol is a set of rules that computers follow to communicate with each other, and they generally involve encryption of some sort. There are lots of protocols, but in the following sections we'll discuss only a few that are the most common.

Point-to-Point Protocol (PPP)

In this protocol, servers are used to validate remote clients before they can access a network. For the most part, this is done using passwords. The password has to be shared between the two in advance. PPP is used to make a direct connection. Connections that use PPP include direct connections such as cell phones, serial cables, phone lines, and dial-up.

Password Authentication Protocol (PAP)

PAP is one of the oldest and weakest protocols. The client sends credentials consisting of a username and password, which are sent as plain text and, thus, vulnerable to attacks. PAP is used as a last resort in networks today. Other protocols are much more secure.

Challenge-Handshake Authentication Protocol (CHAP)

CHAP is more secure than PAP and is sometimes used by Internet service providers (ISPs) to authenticate clients. CHAP can identify the client again and again during a session. A random string is involved in authentication, and both the client and the server must know this string, but the string is never passed over the network.

Extensible Authentication Protocol (EAP)

EAP is more popular than PAP or CHAP and is widely used over the various IEEE networks. It is a general authentication framework for wireless and point-to-point connections and comes in many forms including EAP-TLS and EAP-MD5 among others. EAP encapsulates EAP messages. Encapsulation involves adding a header and (sometimes a) footer to the various layers of a protocol stack and services both the OSI model and the TCP/IP suite of protocols.

Kerberos

Kerberos is the default authentication method for the more recent Microsoft server products including Server 2012. This protocol requires a trusted third party be included in the encryption and decryption of user credentials. This protocol allows secure connections over unsecured networks, such as the Internet.

Viewing Protocol Options on a Windows 10 Client Machine

To see what protocols are available for any Windows-based computer, access the Status dialog box for the active network connection by following these steps:

1. In the Search window on the taskbar, type **Network and Sharing**.

2. Click Network and Sharing in the results.

3. Click the active connection. In Figure 1-3, this is a wireless connection.

4. From the Status dialog box, click the Properties option to the right of Details. (In Figure 1-3 that's Wireless Properties.)

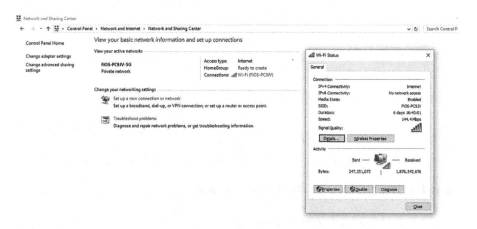

Figure 1-3. *The Status dialog box for the active network*

5. Click the Security tab.

6. Note the settings for the security type and encryption type. Write these down if you plan on making changes here.

7. If you don't see network authentication protocols (not shown in Figure 1-3), change the "Security type" setting to WPA2-Enterprise.

8. Under "Choose a network authentication method," review the protocols available. Figure 1-4 shows an example.

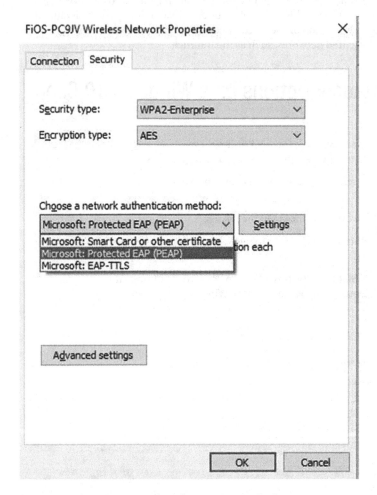

Figure 1-4. Viewing network authentication methods

9. Review any other settings as desired.

10. Click Cancel. Click Close.

■ **Caution** It's important not to make changes to the authentication method without first checking with the network administrator. If the protocols don't match, authorization can't be granted.

IPsec

IPsec is a protocol that works at the network layer of the communications model. IPsec is often used to secure virtual private networks. IPsec provides two security options. Authentication Header (AH) is the first and allows authentication for the sender of data. Encapsulating Security Payload (ESP) is the second, which allows the authentication of the sender but also provides encryption of data.

The specific information involved with this protocol is added to the packet in a header. There are two modes: transport and tunnel. In transport mode, the payload of the packet is usually encrypted or authenticated. In tunnel mode, the entire packet is encrypted and authenticated.

Popular Connection Technologies

When users are sitting at their desk, on-site, they likely use on-site technologies for securing their transmissions. One of the options network administrators configure is to connect via Ethernet, with a direct line to the local router, which connects users to the local intranet and the resources on it. Mechanisms exist on enterprise networks to secure this type of transmission. But when users are out of the office, the on-site options aren't available to them. In these cases, other technologies are used. One popular option is a virtual private network.

VPNs

VPNs allow clients to use shared and public networks to transmit data securely to and from a distant private network, often one an enterprise offers. This enables users to access the company intranet from anywhere, including hotel rooms, conference centers, and coffee shops, safely and securely. To make this possible, a private "tunnel" is created that forms a direct connection between the user and the applicable intranet server. The data that's sent and received through the tunnel is encrypted as well. The server must run the appropriate VPN services to make this happen, and the client must have a VPN connection set up to use it.

Let's take a minute to see how setting up a VPN looks on the client side. If you opt to follow along with the process, you'll be able to see what has to be available for configuration on the server side as well as what needs to be configured on the client. Once the VPN is set up, the connection will appear in the list of available networks on the taskbar (available by clicking the Network icon).

To create a VPN on a Windows 10 client, follow these steps:

1. Click Start and click Settings. It's an icon that looks like a cog or wheel.

2. If you see a back arrow at the top of this window, click it.

3. Click Network & Internet.

4. Click VPN in the left pane. See Figure 1-5.

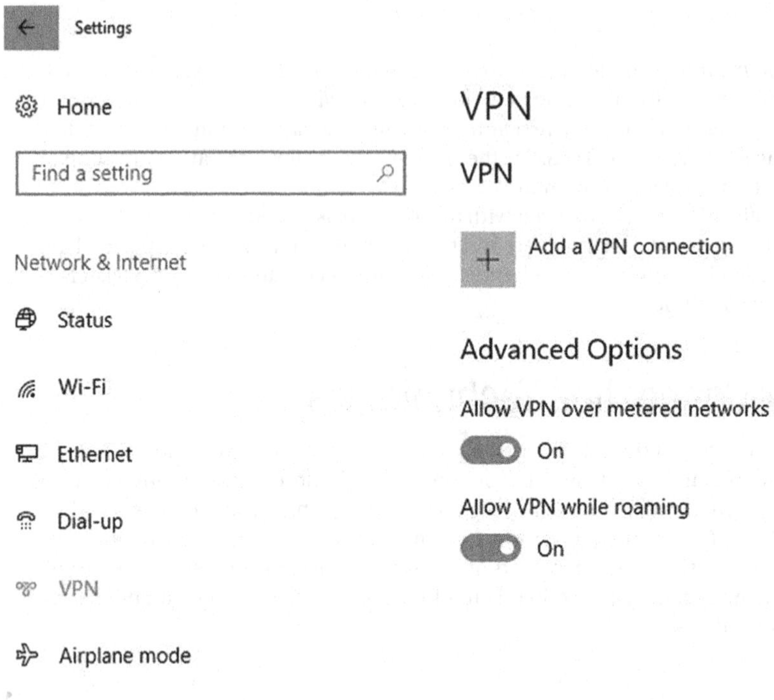

← Settings

⚙ Home

| Find a setting | 🔎 |

Network & Internet

🌐 Status

📶 Wi-Fi

🖥 Ethernet

☎ Dial-up

♈ VPN

✈ Airplane mode

VPN

VPN

➕ Add a VPN connection

Advanced Options

Allow VPN over metered networks

🔘 On

Allow VPN while roaming

🔘 On

Figure 1-5. *The Settings window and VPN options*

5. Click "Add a VPN connection."

6. Work through the wizard, selecting the VPN provider, network name, server name or address, VPN type, type of sign-in, and, optionally, username and password. For the VPN type, select the appropriate protocol. See Figure 1-6.

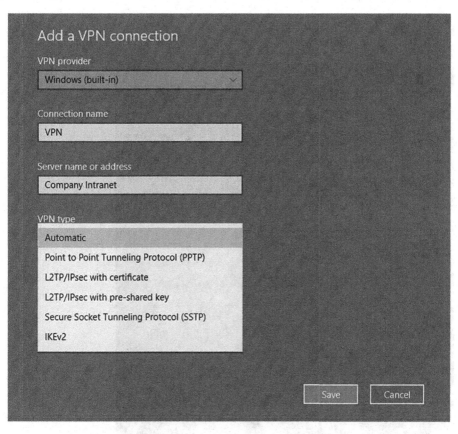

Figure 1-6. *Selecting the protocol type*

7. Click Save.

8. To see the VPN and connect to it, click the Network icon on the taskbar. See Figure 1-7.

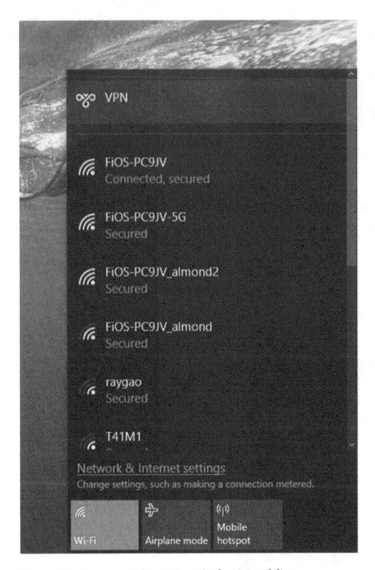

Figure 1-7. New connections appear in the Network list

Workplace Join

There was a time when the only remote connection option corporations gave employees was through company-owned laptops. Administrators would configure those laptops with VPNs or similar technologies and the user would access the enterprise intranet using them. Nowadays, though, with the popularity of bring-your-own-device (BYOD) policies, users need access from their own devices as well. Microsoft addressed this issue with the addition of Workplace Join. Workplace Join works with the Azure Active Directory Device

Registration service to allow users and administrators to create a solution that is both flexible and secure for all involved.

■ **Note**   Windows 8.1, Windows 10, iOS 6.0+, and Android 4.0+ devices use Workplace Join.

Workplace Join offers the following features:

- Uses device authentication to manage known devices.

- Enables administrators to control access to company resources through authentication (and authorization).

- Provides a seamless sign-in experience as well as a single sign-on (SSO) experience. SSO reduces the number of password prompts users encounter.

- Requires Azure Active Directory Device Registration, and administrators must work through the process to configure on-premise conditional access.

Summary

Networks are complex and often vast behemoths, with so many potential bottlenecks and problem areas that it's a wonder we still use them at all. However, they are also the essential glue that holds our businesses and organizations together.

It's those connections that you'll look at in the next chapter. How do you join computers to different types of network, and then how do you manage those connections to ensure stability and a reliable service? These questions and more will be answered.

CHAPTER 2

■ ■ ■

Managing Network Connections

Computer networks come in all shapes and sizes. A network might consist of only three or four desktop or laptop computers configured as a homegroup, or it could consist of hundreds of workstations and dozens of servers in an enterprise. In this chapter, we'll discuss how to work with clients after a network has been configured.

Specifically, we'll focus on understanding and selecting a network profile, seeing the various ways clients will be connecting to wireless networks, managing the networks you connect to, and working with installed network adapters. We'll also discuss creating and managing ad hoc networks and why they are useful.

Understanding Networking Profiles

Before you connect to any network or allow a client to, you must ask yourself one thing first: do you trust the network you want to connect to, or don't you? For nondomain Windows clients, the prompt to make this decision appears after the user clicks the network in the network list and types the appropriate credentials. Once a user answers the question, a network profile is applied. Each profile has specific settings designed to keep the user, the computer, and the computer data safe while connected to that specific network. If the user disconnects and connects again at a later time, that same user profile is applied.

There are three profiles. If the user answers that the network can't be trusted, such as those in coffee shops and hotels, the Public profile is applied. The Public profile might also be referred to as the Guest profile. The Private profile is applied if the user answers that the network is one that can be trusted, such as one in a home or office. There's one more profile, though, which is the Domain profile. The Domain profile is applied when the user logs on to a domain, and those users are not prompted. Let's take a closer look at these profiles and their default settings.

© Mike Halsey and Joli Ballew 2017
M. Halsey and J. Ballew, *Windows Networking Troubleshooting*,
https://doi.org/10.1007/978-1-4842-3222-4_2

Public (or Guest)

The Public profile is designed for public networks. Laptop users connect through these networks when they travel. They might use these networks to play games or get personal e-mail, but if they are using a company laptop, they might also use these networks with a secure VPN to connect to an enterprise domain to access corporate resources. Whatever the case, the Public network profile leaves Network Discovery or File and Print Sharing features disabled to protect the user and the computer. Figure 2-1 shows the Public profile on a Windows 10 client PC.

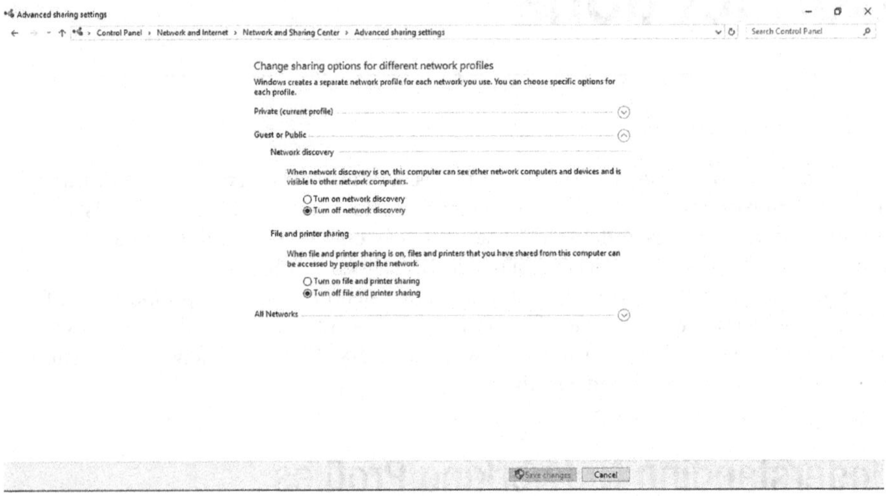

Figure 2-1. *The Public profile's sharing settings*

■ **Note** Network Discovery settings are what determine whether a computer can be seen on the network or whether it is hidden from view. File and Print Sharing settings determine whether files and printers can be seen over the network or whether they are hidden as well.

To access these settings, follow these steps:

1. Right-click the Network icon on the taskbar and click Open Network and Sharing Center.

2. Click Change Advanced sharing settings in the left pane.

3. If applicable, expand the Public profile.

Private

The Private profile is designed for trusted networks. Users connect through these networks when they are on-site in a trusted enterprise or in their own home or small office. The Private network profile leaves Network Discovery disabled at first, and the user is prompted to enable Network Discovery when the need arises, such as the first time they try to access a network resource.

Users might also be prompted to enable File and Print Sharing, depending on how the computer is configured. To see the settings for the Private network profile, refer to Figure 2-1, follow the steps after it, and expand the Private profile.

Domain

If the network adapter on the client machine can find a domain controller and the user can log in, the network profile is set to Domain. In this case, the domain's rules apply. Much of the time, when a user logs into a domain, the user is identified as a specific group member, and that group is given permission to access specific resources on it. Resources can include files, folders, servers, printers, and so on. The domain rules override any rules applied from other profiles or the settings on the computer employee is using.

To see the settings for the Domain network profile, refer to Figure 2-1, follow the steps after it, and expand the Domain profile.

Changing the Network Profile

If you connect to a network and select the Public profile and want to change it to Private, or vice versa, you can. You can't make changes when the Domain profile is active, though.

To change the network profile on a Windows 10 client machine, follow these steps:

1. Click Start and then Settings.

2. If you see a back arrow in the top-left corner, click it.

3. Click Network & Internet.

4. From the Status tab, click Change Connection Properties.

5. Under Make This PC Discoverable, do one of the following:

    a. Move the slider from On to Off to switch from a Private profile to a Public one.

    b. Move the slider from Off to On to switch from a Public profile to a Private one.

Installing Network Support

It's unlikely that you'll have to install basic network support, such as Internet Protocol version 4 (TCP/IPv4) or Internet Protocol version 6 (TCP/IP v6). These protocol stacks are installed by default. However, there are some protocols that not installed including Hyper-V Extensible External Switch and Microsoft Network Adapter Multiplexor Protocol. Figure 2-2 shows this.

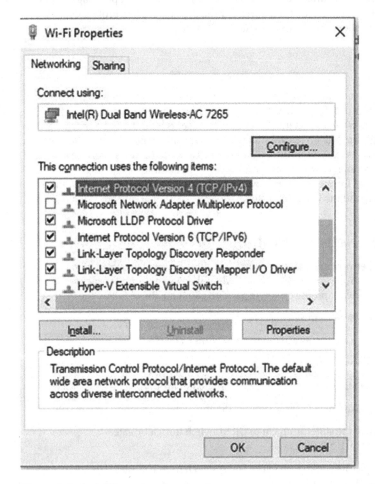

Figure 2-2. *Installing network support*

To get more information about any of these protocols, simply click it in the list. Figure 2-2 shows this information about TCP/IP v4: "Transmission Control Protocol/Internet Protocol. The default wide area network protocol that provides communication across diverse interconnected networks." If you were to click Hyper-V Extensible Virtual Switch, you'd see "Provides network connectivity for virtual machines."

To install (or uninstall) any missing protocol or feature listed here, follow these steps on any Windows machine:

1. Open Control Panel.

2. Click View Network Status and Tasks.

3. Click Change Adapter Settings.

4. Right-click the active network and choose Properties.

5. Select the entry to install or uninstall.

6. Click Install or Uninstall as applicable. See Figure 2-3.

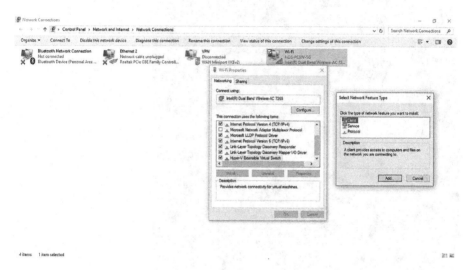

Figure 2-3. *The Properties dialog box for the active network connection*

7. Work through any dialog boxes, which can include installation for Client, Service, or Protocol. See Figure 2-3.

8. When finished, click Close.

Joining a Wireless Network

Windows 10 clients can join a wireless network in multiple ways. The most common is likely from the taskbar's network list. But users can also connect from the Settings window, Control Panel, and even the network adapter's contextual menu. Users can also opt to connect automatically both to known networks and to hotspots. Although connecting to wireless networks is not a highly technical skill, you will be asked as a network administrator to provide support to clients regarding this. Thus, a few pages are dedicated to this topic so that you have multiple options to offer those users.

Using the Network Icon on the Taskbar

The taskbar on a Windows computer includes a Network icon, which can be used to connect to available networks. Figure 2-4 shows the available networks on an example PC. The steps to connect are easy; click the Network icon on the taskbar, click the applicable network, click Connect, and type the credentials. If it's the first time you're connecting, you'll get the trust prompt we talked about earlier. You can opt to enable or disable Network Discovery to tell Windows what network profile to apply. (Enabling Network Discovery applies the Private profile, while disallowing it applies the Public one.)

Figure 2-4. *The Network list available from the taskbar's Network icon*

It's important to note here that while this seems simple enough, users do run into problems when Wi-Fi is disabled or when Airplane Mode is enabled. As you can see in Figure 2-4, the Wi-Fi icon is blue. It's enabled. Airplane Mode is gray. It's disabled. These icons are toggles; simply click to change their status.

Using the Settings Window

The Settings window offers another place to access the network list and connect to networks. Perhaps users won't access this option often, but it's still worth noting. To get there, click Start and then Settings. Click Network & Internet. Click "Show available networks." See Figure 2-5.

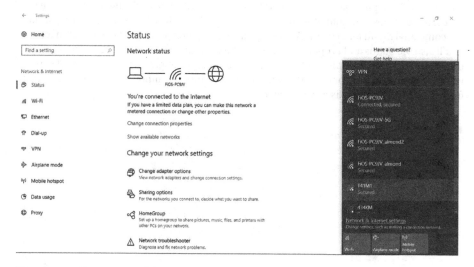

Figure 2-5. *Showing available networks in Settings*

Using Control Panel

Control Panel offers another way to connect to networks, as well as a place to set up a new network. To see these options, open Control Panel, click Network and Internet, and then click Connect to a Network. You'll see the same list as shown in Figure 2-5. However, there are more options here.

- Click View Network Status and Tasks to open the Network and Sharing Center to do the following:

    - Set up new connections

    - Connect to a homegroup or to disconnect from one

    - Troubleshoot a connection

- Click View Network Computers and Devices to access network resources including the following:

  - Computers

  - Network hardware including routers

  - Devices such as media players

  - Printers

Using Adapter Options

Each network adapter, like almost all hardware, includes a contextual menu you can use to access a Properties page and other options, and it's only a right-click away. Figure 2-6 shows the contextual menu for an active Wi-Fi adapter. Notice the option Connect/Disconnect. You'll also see Status and Properties options to explore. If you want to connect and disconnect from a known network from here, you can. This might be a good option if you want to disconnect from one network and connect to another, although you can also do that from the network list we discussed earlier.

Figure 2-6. *A Wi-Fi adapter's contextual menu*

In this example, there's also a VPN, Bluetooth, and Ethernet connection available. These are not active and are not in use, though. These also have contextual menus. In this example, the following (related) options exist via a right-click (although there are others including Properties and Rename):

- *Bluetooth*: In our example, the noteworthy option here is Disable. There's no option to connect or disconnect because there is no available Bluetooth device. If we were connected via Bluetooth, the option to disconnect would exist.

- *Ethernet*: Again, the only option you have is Disable. That's because there's no Ethernet cable connected to this computer. If you connected a cable with an active Ethernet network, the computer would connect automatically, and the option to disconnect would be available. If both Ethernet and Wi-Fi exist, Ethernet is applied.

- *VPN*: The option Connect/Disconnect is available because a VPN has been set up and is available on this PC. You could click Connect/Disconnect to access this network.

Connecting Automatically and Using Metered Connections

When you connect a Windows computer to an Ethernet network (via an Ethernet cable), the connection is made automatically. That's not always true of wireless networks. When you get within range of a wireless network, you may see that a wireless network is available, or you may not. If your computer is in Airplane Mode, you won't, for instance, or if Wi-Fi is disabled. Of course, you won't see a network if there's no wireless network card installed, which is sometimes still the case with desktop computers.

You will be reconnected to known networks automatically (those you've connected to before), if you've configured your computer to do so. There's an option to connect automatically when you first connect to a network. Figure 2-7 shows this option. If you miss this prompt and want to configure your laptop to connect automatically at a later time, you can do so from Settings. We'll show you how shortly.

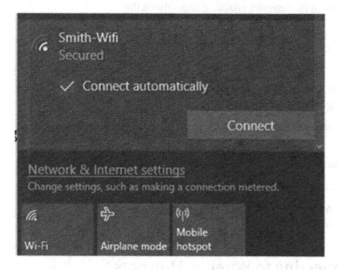

Figure 2-7. *The option to connect automatically to a network*

You can also opt to automatically connect to "suggested open hotspots." This feature used to be referred to as Wi-Fi Sense, and the suggested spots were shared hotspots created by friends, or other options used by your friends, often from Facebook, Outlook, or Skype. You used to get to choose which user groups you wanted to trust. However, now it's an option to simply connect to suggested hotspots, leaving you only the On or Off option without any reference that explains from where those suggestions come.

There's one more thing to consider about known networks, and that's whether they are metered networks. Metered networks require payment of some sort, so it's good to mark those as metered as you run across them.

■ **Note** When going through the steps here for a Windows 10 client, note that we've written them for Windows 10, as it was at the time this book was written. Updates can and do make changes to the interface, though, so be aware what you see here might not always be what you'll see on your own PC.

The best way to decide which options are best for you is to view them. To see how the connection settings are configured on your Windows PC with regard to hotspots and to make changes, follow these steps:

1. Click Start and click Settings.

2. Select Network & Internet.

3. Click Wi-Fi.

4. Under Wi-Fi Services, consider enabling or disabling the following:

   • Find paid plans for suggested open hotspots near me

   • Connect to suggested open hotspots

5. Under Hotspot 2.0 Networks, consider enabling the option "use Online Sign-Up to get connected."

To configure how to manage known networks and metered connections, follow these steps:

1. Click the Network icon on the taskbar.

2. Click the network you're connected to and click Properties.

3. Under Connect Automatically When In Range, make a selection (On or Off).

Finding and Connecting to Wireless Hotspots

You can connect to wireless hotspots in coffee shops and similar places the same way you connect to any network. Open networks appear in the Network list from the taskbar. Oftentimes all you have to do is click the name and click Connect and you're in. If it's the first time you're connecting, though, you'll also be prompted to tell Windows if you trust the network, just as was the case earlier.

Some open networks do require a password, though. One of the local pubs here has a password that's "123456789." To get this password, you have to purchase an adult beverage. However, once you've connected, you can connect again automatically if desired.

There are other types of hotspots to talk about. For instance, you can turn your phone into a wireless hotspot, configure a password, and give that password to friends. All you have to do is enable the hotspot in the Settings area of your phone. Once that's done, users can access it from their own devices, provided you share the password you've configure with them. Figure 2-8 shows a Windows 10 machine with the option to connect to a personal Wi-Fi hotspot created on a phone.

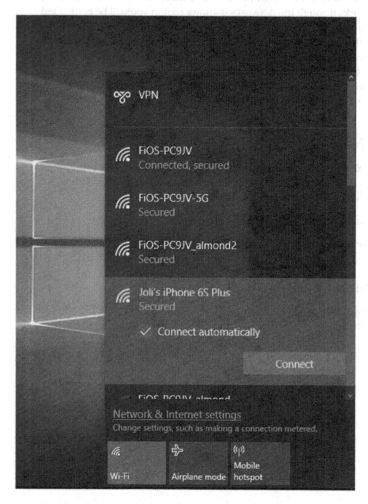

Figure 2-8. Network list with a personal hotspot selected

Managing Wireless Networks

After a while, especially if you travel, you will have connected to a lot of wireless networks. Windows has to remember all of those networks so that you can be connected to them automatically the next time you're within range. Of course, Windows also remembers the network profile it applied the first time you connected, as well as any other settings you've configured since then. Additionally, when you're not connected to a wireless network, Windows regularly works through the networks it knows so that you will be connected when you come within range.

Why does all of this matter? Well, it all causes just a bit of overhead and requires Windows to use system resources when perhaps it isn't necessary. If you take the time to occasionally clear this list of networks you no longer use, you can reduce the work Windows has to do. You can also prioritize your preferred wireless networks and perform other tasks. Let's take a look at clearing that network list first.

Clearing the Network List

Even if you don't think you've connected to a lot of wireless networks, follow the steps here to double-check. If you're using a Windows 8.1 machine, the steps are similar.

To forget unwanted wireless networks, follow these steps:

1. Click Start and then click Settings.

2. Select Network & Internet.

3. Click Wi-Fi in the left pane.

4. Click Manage Known Networks.

5. Select any network and click Forget to remove it from the list. See Figure 2-9.

Figure 2-9. Forgetting a network option in Settings

6.   Repeat step if required for any other networks.

■ **Note**   If you opt to forget a network, the next time you access it you'll get that trust prompt again. It'll be as if you never connected. If you're having trouble configuring settings for a network, consider forgetting it and reconnecting.

Prioritizing Preferred Wireless Networks

Sometimes multiple networks exist in a single home or office, and generally, one is faster than the other. As an example, I have my 5G network and two Wi-Fi extenders in my office. I prefer to connect to the 5G network because I get better connectivity and faster speeds. When more than one network option exists, you can prioritize which Windows attempts to connect to first. However, there's no option to do this inside Control Panel or Settings.

To configure network priority, you must use a command prompt. Here's how:

1. Locate the name associated with your Wi-Fi adapter by doing the following:

   a. Right-click the Network icon on the taskbar.

   b. Click Open Network and Sharing Center.

   c. Select Change Adapter Settings.

   d. Locate the active adapter and write down its name. (Ours is Wi-Fi.)

2. From the taskbar, search for **Command Prompt**.

3. Right-click Command Prompt in the results and select "Run as administrator." See Figure 2-10.

Figure 2-10. Opening the command prompt with administrator privileges

1.   Type **netsh wlan show profiles**. See Figure 2-11.

```
Administrator: Command Prompt
Microsoft Windows [Version 10.0.15063]
(c) 2017 Microsoft Corporation. All rights reserved.

C:\WINDOWS\system32>netsh wlan show profiles

Profiles on interface Wi-Fi:

Group policy profiles (read only)
---------------------------------
    <None>

User profiles
-------------
    All User Profile     : FiOS-PC9JV
    All User Profile     : FiOS-PC9JV-5G
    All User Profile     : COPguest
    All User Profile     : FiOS-PC9JV_almond2
    All User Profile     : mvp2016


C:\WINDOWS\system32>
```

Figure 2-11. *Showing network profiles list*

2.   Note the name of the network connection to make the highest priority. (Ours is FiOS-PC9JV-5G.)

3.   Type **set profileorder name="type *network name here*"
interface="*type adapter name here*" priority=1** and press
Enter on the keyboard.

The netsh command is quite useful and offers additional options for working with networks. We'll discuss netsh in greater detail later in this chapter.

Viewing Network and Hardware Properties

There are occasions where you need to see the properties associated with your connected network and the hardware you use to connect to it. The information includes things such as the SSID, protocol, security type, physical address, and so on. Although there are various ways to retrieve this information, including using commands such as `ipconfig /all` both in PowerShell and at the command prompt, it's quite easy to get that information quickly from the Settings window.

To access basic information about your network and hardware, follow these steps:

1. Click Start, Settings, and then Network & Internet.

2. Select Wi-Fi in the left pane.

3. Click Hardware Properties.

4. Review the information, noting that there's an option to copy it to the clipboard, and then click the Back arrow.

5. Leave this window open for the next section.

Using Random Hardware Addresses

Random hardware addresses make it more difficult for people to track your location when you connect to different Wi-Fi networks. You can make your Windows computer use random hardware addresses for all of your new connections by simply moving the toggle for the setting from Off to On. You'll find that setting in the Settings window, under Network & Internet, on the Wi-Fi tab. See Figure 2-12.

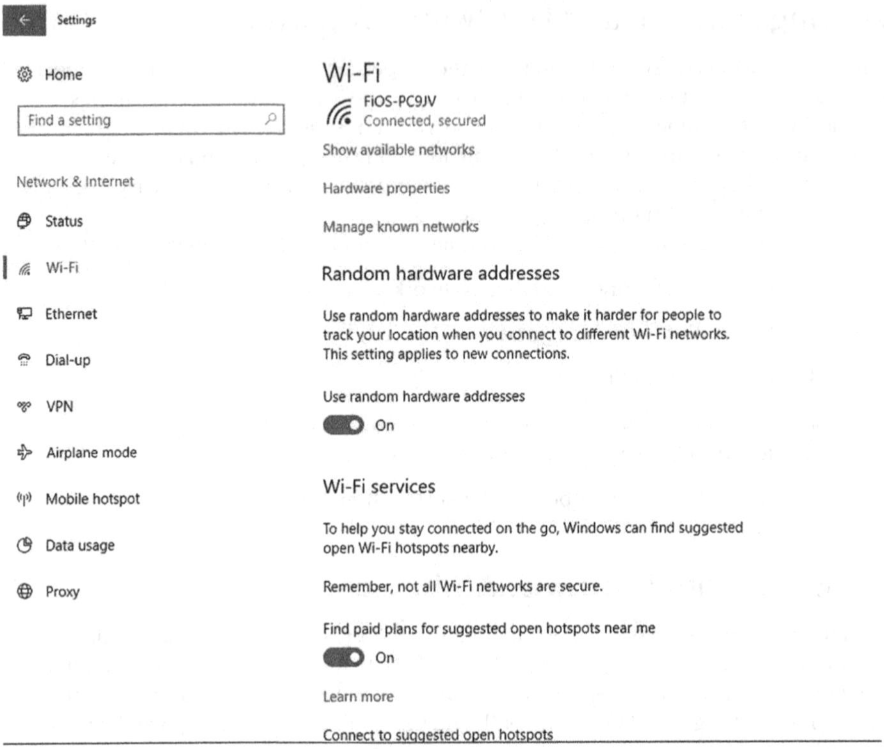

Settings

⚙ Home

Find a setting 🔍

Network & Internet

🖧 Status

📶 Wi-Fi

🖵 Ethernet

☎ Dial-up

⧉ VPN

✈ Airplane mode

(ɪ) Mobile hotspot

🕔 Data usage

🌐 Proxy

Wi-Fi

📶 FiOS-PC9JV
Connected, secured

Show available networks

Hardware properties

Manage known networks

Random hardware addresses

Use random hardware addresses to make it harder for people to track your location when you connect to different Wi-Fi networks. This setting applies to new connections.

Use random hardware addresses

🔵 On

Wi-Fi services

To help you stay connected on the go, Windows can find suggested open Wi-Fi hotspots nearby.

Remember, not all Wi-Fi networks are secure.

Find paid plans for suggested open hotspots near me

🔵 On

Learn more

Connect to suggested open hotspots

Figure 2-12. *The option to use random hardware addresses*

■ **Note** To apply random hardware addresses to older connections, forget any existing connections as detailed earlier and reconnect. The new settings will be applied.

Creating Personal Mobile Hotspots

Finally, there's one other Wi-Fi setting to introduce, and this is the option to use your Windows computer to create a personal mobile hotspot you can share with others. Like other Wi-Fi options, it's available in the Settings window. Figure 2-13 shows this. Once you enable this setting, you have the option to edit the name, password, and network band.

Figure 2-13. *Enabling a Wi-Fi hotspot*

Exploring netsh Commands

You learned a little about the netsh command earlier when we discussed prioritizing networks. That command is powerful and deserves a little more discussion before moving on. Open a command prompt with elevated privileges and try these commands:

- netsh wlan show interfaces: Offers the network name, GUID, physical address, connection mode, authentication type, and more (see Figure 2-14)

■ Administrator: Command Prompt

```
C:\WINDOWS\system32>netsh wlan show interface

There is 1 interface on the system:

    Name                   : Wi-Fi
    Description            : Intel(R) Dual Band Wireless-AC 7265
    GUID                   : 77c658c7-c5c7-42af-8144-a6e9f79185c7
    Physical address       : a4:02:b9:6b:0f:62
    State                  : connected
    SSID                   : FiOS-PC9JV
    BSSID                  : c8:a7:0a:94:19:5a
    Network type           : Infrastructure
    Radio type             : 802.11n
    Authentication         : WPA2-Personal
    Cipher                 : CCMP
    Connection mode        : Auto Connect
    Channel                : 1
    Receive rate (Mbps)    : 144.4
    Transmit rate (Mbps)   : 144.4
    Signal                 : 99%
    Profile                : FiOS-PC9JV

    Hosted network status  : Not available


C:\WINDOWS\system32>netsh wlan show networks

Interface name : Wi-Fi
There are 1 networks currently visible.
```

Figure 2-14. *Using netsh to view interfaces*

- netsh wlan show networks: Displays the SSID for the current network, network type, authentication, and encryption details

- netsh wlan show profiles: Displays the user profiles for all available networks

- netsh wlan show profiles name=<input profile name here>: Offers profile information, connectivity settings, security settings, and cost settings

- netsh wlan show settings: Shows blocked networks, hosted network mode, whether shared user credentials are allowed, and more

Once you get to know these commands, you can start to build longer ones and work with wireless networks from a command line if desired. There are netsh commands available for more than just networks, though, and they include options for the following technologies and features (this is not a complete list):

- IPsec

- Network Policy Server

- Remote access

- Routing

- Windows Firewall

- Windows Firewall with Advanced Security
- Wired local networks

Joining a Virtual Private Network

Network administrators create VPNs to allow users to securely access the enterprise network while away from the office. Specifically, administrators want to create an environment where employees can use the Internet to access the intranet using the Internet as a medium for transmission. Once a VPN is available and has been configured for use on the client machine, the user connects to it the same way they connect to any network, through the network list. Figure 2-15 shows this option. The user will be prompted for credentials.

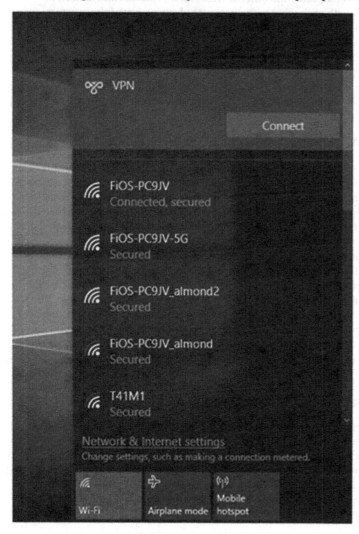

Figure 2-15. *The option to connect to a VPN*

■ **Note**   *Virtual* means that something doesn't exist physically, even though it can appear to and can seem quite real. You might have heard the terms *virtual reality*, *virtual machine*, or *virtual assistant.* These aren't genuine things; they are made possible by software. The same is true of virtual private networks. They are networks that are made possible by software, protocols, and so forth, and appear to be, at least to the user, very real.

Understanding Ad Hoc Networks

Ad hoc networks allow computers and other devices (such as phones and tablets) to communicate directly with each other without the use of any network infrastructure. Infrastructure generally consists of hardware such as routers and access points. There's none of this in an ad hoc network, and there are also no central servers, domain controllers, or any other type of interim devices that deal with data transfer.

There are two types of ad hoc networks that we'll discuss here: wired and wireless. Note that for a device to participate, it must have the required network hardware and installed protocols. Thus, devices must include a network adapter.

Using Wired Ad Hoc Networks

For a device to participate in a wired ad hoc network, it needs to have a network card with an Ethernet port (or a way to create an Ethernet port). Newer devices like tablets and laptops might not come with this built in. There are options, though; you could install a USB-to-Ethernet adapter if Ethernet is the only way to communicate with a designated device. Once connected, the two devices can communicate. Often the purpose is to share files quickly.

Microsoft, at one time, required you to create an ad hoc network if you wanted to move data from an older Windows 7 computer to a new one running Windows 8 by using the Windows Easy Transfer Wizard. This program came with Windows 7. Microsoft sold a cable specifically for this. The cable was called a Windows 7 Easy Transfer Cable. In reality, though, this was just a crossover cable. To use such a cable, you simply connected the cable to both computers' Ethernet ports and configured the proper sharing options on each device. These types of networks are still available today; however, it is more likely users will set up wireless ad hoc networks now.

Using Wireless Ad Hoc Networks

You know already that for two devices to connect to each other they must both have networking hardware. Additionally, though, a device must also be able to support a hosted network, which means being able to implement the wireless hosted network service. The hosted network service was first made available in Windows 7 and Server 2008 R2, but again, the hardware must support it for devices to be able to implement it. If a hardware manufacturer wants its device to meet hosted network requirements, its network adapter driver must include support for this feature.

How does this work? With the hosted network service and required hardware available, a Windows computer can use its physical wireless adapter to perform two tasks at once. It can connect as a client to a hardware access point (AP) for its own connectivity, while concurrently serving as a software AP allowing other devices to connect through it.

How can you tell whether your computer meets the requirements and a hosted network is allowed? You need to run a few commands at the command line. Here's how:

1. Open a command prompt with elevated privileges.

2. Type **netsh wlan show drivers**.

3. Locate the "Hosted network supported" status line. See Figure 2-16. In this example, a hosted network is either not (yet) supported or the service hasn't yet been allowed.

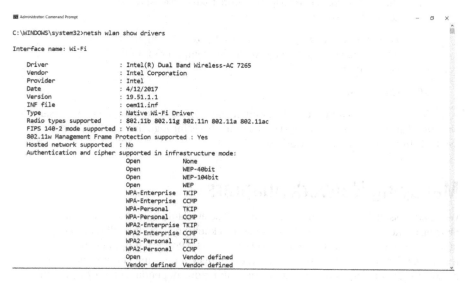

Figure 2-16. Hosted network support entry

4. To see whether you can allow the computer to provide a hosted network, type this command: **netsh wlan set hostednetwork mode=allow ssid=network name key=password**. The *network name* is the name of your network; the *password* is the network password. See Figure *2-17*.

■ Administrator: Command Prompt

```
C:\WINDOWS\system32>netsh wlan set hostednetwork mode=allow ssid=FiOS-PC9JV key=nut8857dim9164site
The hosted network mode has been set to allow.
The SSID of the hosted network has been successfully changed.
The user key passphrase of the hosted network has been successfully changed.


C:\WINDOWS\system32>
```

Figure 2-17. Allowing a hosted network

5. Open the Network and Sharing Center.

6. Click Change Adapter Settings.

7. Right-click the active adapter if more than one exists and select Properties.

8. From the sharing tab, select the check box allow other network users to connect through this computer's internet connection.

9. Click Close.

The connection is now available for other users. Users access the network the same way they'd access any network. Most of the time, this is through the list of networks available from the taskbar's Network icon.

Managing Network Adapters

We've addressed the Change Adapter Settings link, available from the Network and Sharing Center, several times in this chapter. You know you can right-click any adapter in the list to access a contextual menu. There's always a Properties option, and as you learned earlier, there might also be options to connect or disconnect from a network, disable the adapter, diagnose the connection, and more, depending on the device and whether it's connected to a network. We have yet to discuss the properties associated with the actual adapter itself, though.

To explore your own network adapter's specific properties, follow these steps:

1. Navigate to Control Panel, select Network and Internet, and then select Network Connections.

2. Right-click the active adapter and click Properties.

3. Click Configure. See Figure 2-18.

Figure 2-18. *A network adapter's Properties dialog box*

What you see now is dependent on the adapter you select. For example, our Ethernet adapter's Properties box has seven tabs.

- General

- Advanced

- About

- Driver

- Details

- Events

- Power Management

But our wireless adapter has only five (see Figure 2-19).

- General

- Advanced

- Driver

- Events

- Power Management

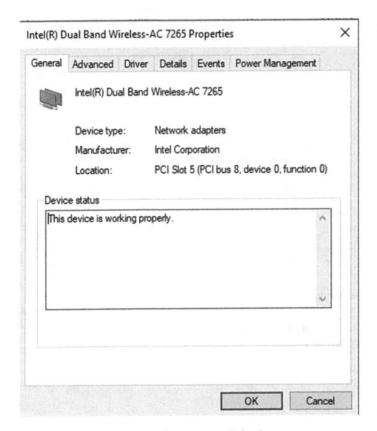

Figure 2-19. *A Wi-Fi adapter's Properties dialog box*

You'll use a few of the tabs more than others, if you use them at all. We'll discuss the most common tabs next, but feel free to review any not covered here on your own. Tabs such as General and About, for example, don't offer anything to configure and thus don't offer much to talk about.

Advanced

The Advanced tab lists the network adapter properties and any values associated with them. Often there are multiple choices for a given property. However, don't make changes here unless you know exactly what you're doing. You could render the device unusable with the wrong settings.

Here are a few examples of what you might find on this tab:

- *Transmit Power*: Options range from lowest to highest. Highest is often the default.

- *Wireless Mode*: Options can include 802.11a, 8002.11b, 802.11g, and 802.11a/b/g.

Driver

The Driver tab offers what you'll see when you access the device through Device Manager. This is where you troubleshoot a network adapter. From this tab you can update and roll back a driver, disable the device, and even uninstall the device.

Events

The Events tab lists important dates associated with the device and its driver. You might see entries for when the driver service was added and when the device was installed. You'll see a new entry under Events if you update a device driver from the Driver tab. This entry will be another Device Installed entry.

Power Management

The Power Management tab for almost all wireless adapters lets you configure at least two settings.

- "Allow the computer to turn off this device to save power"

- "Allow this device to wake the computer"

Configure these settings as you see fit. Generally, the default is to leave the first option enabled and the second disabled, but it's ultimately your call.

Summary

Managing network connections involves many areas of expertise. In this chapter, you learned about several of them. First, when discussing networks, you must decide whether the network you want to connect to is a public network or a private one. You're deciding whether you'll trust the network. The decision you make tells Windows what network profile to apply (Public or Private). There's also a Domain profile for enterprise users. Also, to use a network, the required protocols must be installed, and for the most part they are. There are some older protocols, as well as specialty protocols, that can be installed when the need arises.

There are various kinds of networks too, including wireless, VPNs, and ad hoc. We covered how to set them up, connect to them, and manage them. You learned with wireless networks, at least, that you should keep an eye on the network list, especially if you travel. It's important to cull that list of unwanted networks periodically and prioritize the networks you do use.

Finally, you learned how to work with hardware and network profiles and manage network adapters. Some of these options are included in the Settings app and are easy to access. Others require you to access the Properties page of the adapter or connection.

CHAPTER 3

■ ■ ■

TCP/IP Networking

Networks exist to enable computer users to do their work and communicate with others. Thus, networking is one of the primary functions of any operating system. There are various kinds of networks.

Most general consumers connect to the Internet through a home router and share that connection (and perhaps a printer or two) with other users on the network. A small, local area network (LAN) like this also enables users to share files and media, mostly to make the data available to everyone who requires access.

Many large companies create and use networks for similar reasons but on a broader scale. These larger networks use routers just like home users, but they can also include Active Directory servers, print and mail servers, wired and wireless extenders, and more. These types of resources can be used to securely connect devices and users to both the enterprise network and the Internet. Active Directory servers (among other things) can be used to make resources available to those who have the proper permissions as well.

All networks can include computers that run differing operating systems. In an enterprise, for instance, members in the accounting department might use Windows-based devices, while members of the art department might use Apple-based ones. There could even be a few Linux machines in the mix. Additionally, some users will connect via Ethernet, while others will use mobile devices and connect wirelessly (such as iPads and Surface Pros).

The art of networking lies in the ability for all devices to communicate with each other (no matter their OS or hardware type) and provide the desired services to users.

So, the question becomes, how do all of these devices communicate? What technologies must exist for, say, wired Apple computers to communicate with wireless Microsoft tablets? Beyond that, how do IPv4, IPv6, DHCP, and DNS play a role? That's what we'll talk about in this chapter.

Exploring the Layers of the OSI Model

Computer networking requires that computers and devices communicate with each other using existing protocols (rules) that manufacturers agree to implement to make their devices interoperable with others. Without rules, no piece of hardware would be able to communicate with another reliably, if at all. The Open Systems Interconnection (OSI) reference model was created and is the independent standard that computer manufacturers have agreed to implement to advance this interoperability.

© Mike Halsey and Joli Ballew 2017
M. Halsey and J. Ballew, *Windows Networking Troubleshooting*,
https://doi.org/10.1007/978-1-4842-3222-4_3

To make understanding the OSI model easier, the protocols used are separated into seven distinct layers. These are stacked one on top of the other when described, and they detail how data is modified and transitioned to be moved successfully among devices and across networks and the Internet. These layers form a stack and include TCP/IP protocols at the network layer, which is why it's called the TCP/IP stack. The bottommost layer is the Physical layer.

Physical Layer

The Physical layer details the protocols required to transmit data across physical mediums. This layer represents all the hardware that forms a network. Think about the possibilities! There are wired and wireless network interface adapters, radio signals and Ethernet cables for transmission, telephone jacks and their related cables, USB ports, wired and wireless extenders, switches, hubs, servers, workstations of all kinds, and more. Each of these resources has a manufacturer as well as unique physical hardware. Figure 3-1 shows one network adapter manufacturer, but imagine how many more there are. You can see information like this from Device Manager.

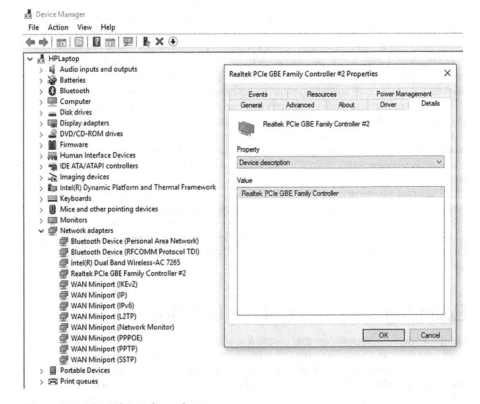

Figure 3-1. *Network interface adapter*

For the myriad of possible devices to communicate, all must agree to use the protocols associated with the Physical layer as detailed by the OSI model. Specifically, devices need to agree on how the bits of data will be moved. Within this architecture, the Physical layer transmits logical communications requests both to and from the Data-Link layer, which is the layer above it. These communications are hardware-specific operations. This enables the transmission or reception of electronic signals to and from devices. The other layers work via software. This is the only physical layer.

Data-Link Layer

While the Physical layer of the OSI model deals with physical devices, as noted, the rest of the layers exist as software only. To understand what the Data-Link layer does and how it does it, though, you need to know a little about how data is passed from one device to another first.

Data that is transmitted across networks is separated into small, transmittable packets. Most Windows networks are called *packet-switching networks* for this reason. For example, a single e-mail might be separated into thousands of packets, each containing a small piece of the message. It's not possible to send a message like this as a single unit. The packets arrive at their destination, often at different times and from varying routes, and must be reassembled once they arrive. The Data-Link layer is responsible for putting those pieces back together at the destination computer.

For this technology to work, each packet must include information about what it contains, where it is from, and where it is going, among other things. During the progression, each packet goes through a process of data encapsulation, where a frame is added to it. That frame contains a header and a footer that holds the required information for this layer to function. This includes the hardware addresses of the devices (media access control addresses). It also includes information about the protocol used as well as a way to regulate whether the data has been manipulated on the way. As the data continues to move through layers, more information is added. Each layer has a purpose.

■ **Note**   Several protocols are supported at this layer including but not limited to Address Resolution Protocol (ARP), Ethernet, IEEE 802.11, and Token Ring.

Network Layer

The Network layer is the next layer up the OSI stack. This layer is responsible for IP addressing, routing, and subnet masking. This is a complex topic, and entire books are available on each of these subjects. Briefly, though, the unique protocols used here are Transmission Control Protocol/Internet Protocol (TCP/IP).

To understand how TCP/IP fits in, let's talk about those packets again. In the Data-Link layer, Ethernet is generally used to move data along a wired local area network. This is one unique example of how data can travel, though. However, the point here is that this is a LAN protocol. To move data packets across dissimilar networks, the data packets must pass through a router. IP is the protocol used to do this. IP is called an *end-to-end protocol* for this reason; it takes data from one end of the spectrum to the other. Like the previous layer, this layer adds information as well, but in the form of a header.

The header includes the packets' source and destination IP addresses, among other things, including protocol information. The data is then passed to the Transport layer.

For this layer to work, each computer must have its TCP/IP protocol stack configured correctly. This means having the proper TCP/IP protocols (as well as others) installed, as detailed in Chapter 2. You install the protocols from the Properties dialog box for the active network adapter, as shown in Figure 3-2. As you can see here, there are protocols for IPv4 and IPv6 as well as others.

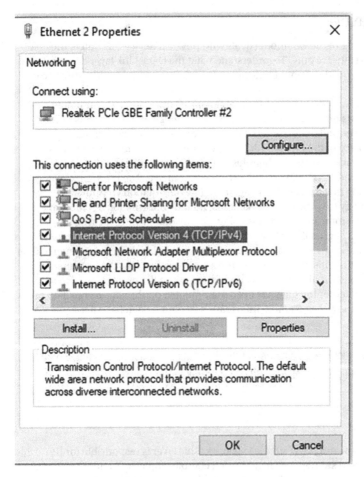

Figure 3-2. *Ethernet Properties dialog box*

Transport Layer

The Transport layer and the Network layer share some properties and technologies, even though we distinguish them as two separate entities when we explain the OSI model. Both incorporate two additional protocols, connection-oriented and connectionless, to describe how the device will, well, connect to other devices. The protocol must be agreed on by both parties, the sender and the receiver, before any data is transmitted.

In a *connection-oriented* network, the two devices agree that perfect data transmission is a necessity. Although this involves lots of overhead, it is necessary for data that must arrive with no errors, such as data in a software download or data sent to and from devices in an operating room. This type of data must arrive intact and perfect, or it must be re-sent.

With a *connectionless* protocol, it's okay if some of the data bits are lost along the way. Think about streaming video. It's alright if a few bits get lost. It's even okay if the data pixelates a bit because lots of bits are lost.

As with previous layers, in this layer another header is added to the frame. It includes information about ports and sockets, among other things. The port details what protocol is used. Port 80 is HTTP, for instance, while port 110 is POP3. The receiving computer needs this information once it arrives so it'll know what application should be used to open it. When you combine the port with the IP address, you get what's called a *socket*. As an example, a socket number of 192.168.4.2:80 represents the destination IP address of 192.168.4.2, while the 80 following it means that the destination computer needs to use something that can handle the HTTP protocol. It's HTTP data.

Additionally, data encapsulation at this layer includes TCP and User Datagram Protocol (UDP) information. This details what will happen if a packet doesn't make it to its destination. Will lost packets be re-sent, or will they be ignored? All of this and more work to make this layer function.

Upper Layers (Session, Presentation, Application)

Finally, there are three upper layers. We are grouping these together here because they are all related to what happens once the data has been sent across the network and appears at the destination computer.

First, understand that the data packets must be "unencapsulated." The networking stack on the receiving computer has to work through the same layers but backward to extract the information required to complete the delivery of the data. Once that data is ready, the computer accepts the data, and then programs installed on the computer take control from there.

For example, if you think about e-mail, for instance, it's an e-mail application such as Microsoft Outlook that handles presenting the data to the client. (It could be an e-mail server.) If it's information from the Internet, it's Microsoft Edge, Firefox, or Chrome, perhaps. Applications don't know about any protocols, though; they don't know if you're on a local network or an enterprise, and they don't care. They are responsible only for offering the data to the user.

Understanding the Dual Stack

Earlier we discussed the Network layer, and you learned that this is the layer of the OSI model that handles IP addressing. This includes IPv4 and IPv6, among others. We aren't here to teach you how to decipher these IP addresses; that could take several chapters. Instead, we'd like to address the idea of the dual stack.

Briefly, a *dual stack* is a TCP/IP stack that is capable of working with both IPv4 and IPv6 addresses at the same time and can originate and decipher both types of packets. Let's take a minute to review these protocols.

IPv4 Addressing

You might remember that in the early days of the Internet a group of scientists and engineers got together and created the IPv4 system. IPv4 addresses were created with both a network identifier and a host identifier and were 32 bits long. The network part defined the destination network; the host part defined the specific host on that network. Each node on a network must have a unique IP address so that data can be sent to it. (It's just like having an address assigned to your home. It must be unique to your city so the mail carrier can deliver your mail.)

IPv4 addressing uses a Base 2 system, incorporating only 1s and 0s grouped together in four octets. Those octets are converted to Base 10 so that we, as humans, can work with them more easily. For example, an IP address of 00101111.10111000.10101101.11010000 would translate to 47.184.173.208. If you're interested in converting IP addresses to Base 10, there are several online conversion tools available.

Anyway, although it seemed at the time that this type of system would last forever, we've run out of IPv4 addresses. Thus, IPv6 was created to address the shortage.

IPv6 Addressing

IPv6 uses a hexadecimal system. These addresses are 16 bytes long (versus 128 bits) and are formed with eight 2-byte values. Here's an example of an IPv6 address: 2001:0db8:85a3: 0000:0000:8a2e:0370:7334.

Using this system, each entry can have a value from 0 to 9 and a letter from A to F. Thus, one 8-bit number can have 256 values. If you can imagine it, there are 3.4×10^{38}, or 340 undecillion, available IPv6 addresses. In theory, we should never run out. If you recall, though, there was a time we thought we'd never run out of IPv4 addresses!

IPv6 Transition

IPv4 is alive and well. Just because there aren't any more unique addresses doesn't mean that we're all going to stop using the IPv4 infrastructure. All computers still support IPv4, and they will for some time. The Internet runs on it. But computers must also be able to process and deal with IPv6 addresses when required. At some point, there will be a desire by most to transition to IPv6 from all angles. So, how is the world planning on handling this transition?

As you might imagine, this transition is complicated. Mechanisms have to be in place to let this transition happen gradually, while still incorporating IPv4 successfully.

Let's take a brief look at some of the available technologies companies are implementing to make the transition:

- *Native IPv6*: This is a network that relies solely on IPv6. This isn't going to work just yet but is a valid, albeit lofty, goal for enterprise intranets.

- *Dual stack*: This is a network that uses IPv6 when it can and uses IPv4 as a fallback when required.

- *Tunneling*: This is a network that wants to use IPv6 as much as possible but encapsulates IPv6 into an IPv4 network when required. 6-4 is a tunneling technique, as are 6RD, ISATAP, and Teredo.

Using DHCP

Dynamic Host Configuration Protocol (DHCP) is a means to assign IP addresses to nodes on a network. As you know, each host or node has to have its own unique IP address.

DHCP is a protocol that enables nodes on a network to obtain their IP address automatically. In large enterprises, addresses often come from a pool of addresses stored on a DHCP server. Addresses are obtained and released as clients need them. Windows computers, including Windows 8.1 and Windows 10, come with DHCP abilities built in. Earlier OSs did too, but we'll assume you've moved up from Windows 7 to a more recent OS. To use DHCP, it must be enabled on the client, which is the default setting. However, it's always good to know how to get there and what the DHCP settings look like.

To configure DHCP on a client, follow these steps:

1. Open the Network and Sharing Center.

2. Click Change Adapter Settings.

3. Right-click the active network adapter and click Properties.

4. Click Internet Protocol Version 4 (IPv4) and then click Properties.

5. From the General tab, select "Obtain an IP address automatically." See Figure 3-3.

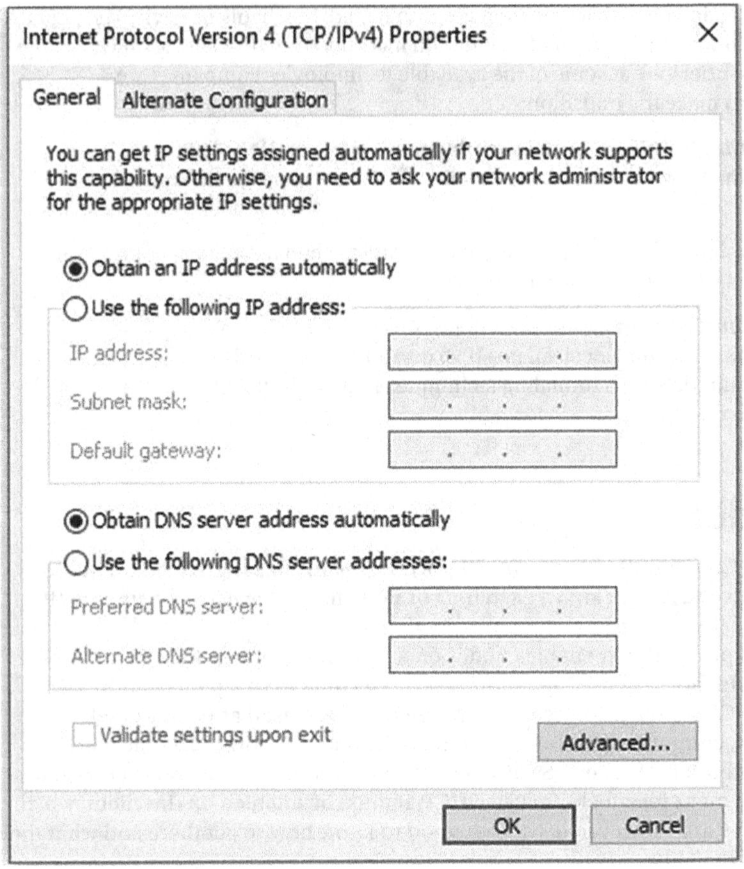

Internet Protocol Version 4 (TCP/IPv4) Properties   ✕

General   Alternate Configuration

You can get IP settings assigned automatically if your network supports this capability. Otherwise, you need to ask your network administrator for the appropriate IP settings.

◉ Obtain an IP address automatically

○ Use the following IP address:

   IP address:

   Subnet mask:

   Default gateway:

◉ Obtain DNS server address automatically

○ Use the following DNS server addresses:

   Preferred DNS server:

   Alternate DNS server:

☐ Validate settings upon exit   Advanced...

OK   Cancel

Figure 3-3. *Using DHCP for IPv4*

6.   Click OK to return to the adapter's Properties dialog box.

7.   Click Internet Protocol Version 6 (IPv6).

8.   Click Properties.

9.   Select "Obtain an IPv6 address automatically." See Figure 3-4.

10.   Click OK.

11.   Click Close.

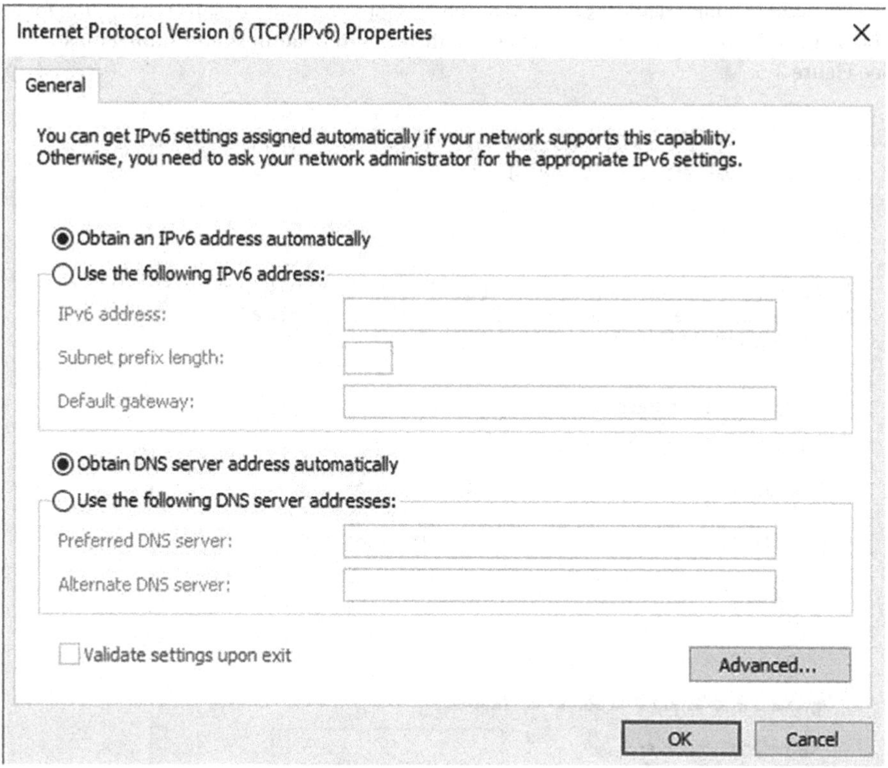

Figure 3-4. *Using DHCP for IPv6*

Here are some additional benefits of DHCP:

- Minimizes typographical errors.

- Prevents address conflicts.

- Provides a centralized and automated addressing system that (virtually) never needs attention.

- Offers a simple way to provide addressing for clients that move around a lot, such as mobile computers.

- Provides complete control over the addressing processing including the range of addresses available.

- Forwards DHCP messages using a relay agent. There's no need for a DHCP server on every subnet of a network.

Network administrators can assign an address manually when DHCP won't work. Sometimes this is a good option for hardware that doesn't require (or perhaps support) a dynamic address, such as an older printer, but is more often applied to devices that simply can't use DHCP.

To assign a manual address, return to the previous steps and deselect the option to obtain an address automatically. Then, input the desired IP address and subnet mask. See Figure 3-5.

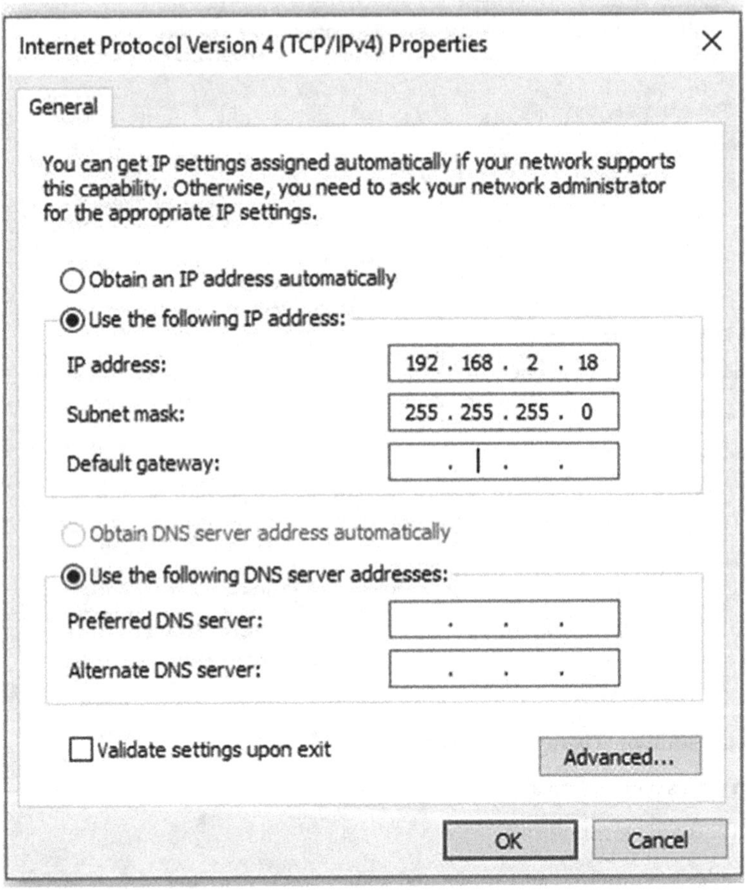

Figure 3-5. Assigning an IP address manually

Understanding DNS

All computers have a unique IP address on their network. That address might look like 192.168.15.25 or 2001:0db8:85a3:0000:0000:8a2e:0370:7334. To connect to a specific computer, using these addresses like these would be cumbersome and error-prone. That's why Domain Name System (DNS) and DNS servers exist. It is a name resolution service. It allows you to input a computer name and get to a computer address. You use DNS each time you enter a web site name in the address bar of a web browser.

Briefly, the DNS server process looks like this when used to access a web site on the Internet:

1. A user types a web site name into a web browser. The browser sends a query over the Internet, seeking to match the name to an IP address.

2. The query makes its way to a recursive server. This server makes a decision about to do next by looking at the name of the web site the user is searching for. It forwards the request to another server that can make the next decision.

3. The next server is called a *root server*. This server looks at the end of the query, such as .com or .edu, and decides where to send the query next. The information is passed along to another server that knows about that root domain.

4. The next server looks at the middle part of the web site name. If the site name is www.wellbeingstx.com, it'll look for wellbeingstx.

5. Once at the server that has information about that domain, information is obtained about the first part of the address, often www.

6. Once there, the web site appears in the web browser.

Some users and network administrators change their default DNS server address manually. A single user might opt to use Google's DNS servers, for example. Two of those addresses are 8.8.8.8 and 2001:4860:4860::8888. A large corporation might have its own DNS servers and want to use those. Whatever the case, it's possible to manually enter a DNS server in a similar manner to configuring DHCP.

To assign a specific IPv4 DNS server to a Windows 10 client (and IPv6 is similar), follow these steps:

1. Open the Network and Sharing Center.

2. Click Change Adapter Settings.

3. Right-click the active network adapter and click Properties.

4. Click Internet Protocol Version 4 (IPv4) and then click Properties.

5. Select "Use the following DNS server addresses."

6. Input the desired address. See Figure 3-6.

7. Click OK.

8. Click Close.

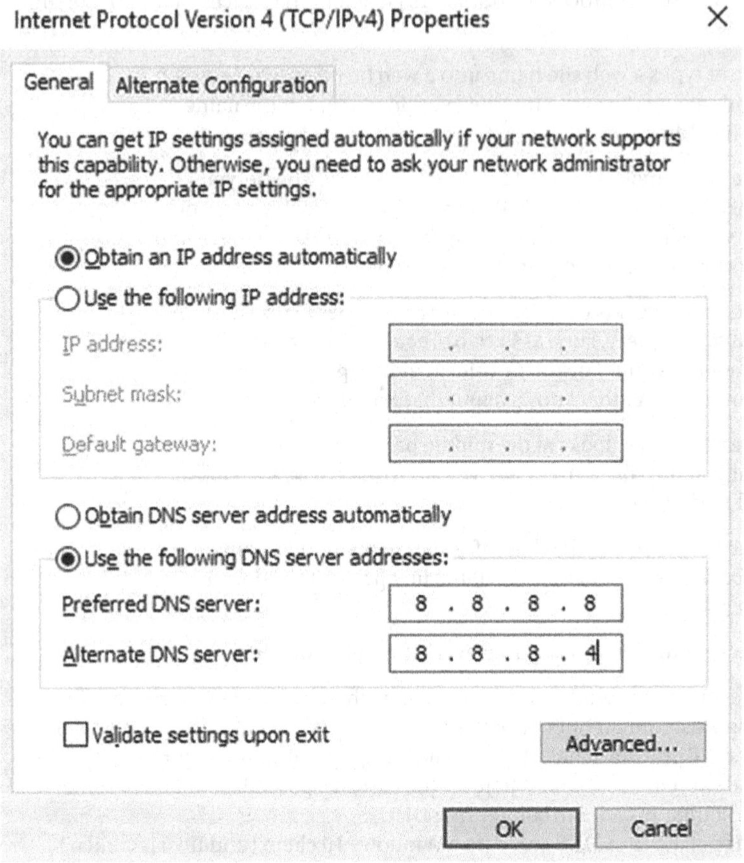

Figure 3-6. *Assigning a static DNS server address*

Troubleshooting Connections with Common TCP/IP Tools

Sometimes problems occur within networks that keep computers and other resources from communicating with each other effectively. After you've checked the most common problems including server outages, broken cables, disabled adapters, malfunctioning cables, downed DHCP servers (perhaps when Automatic Private IP Addressing has been enabled to provide limited communications), blocked wireless signals, and so forth, you can try the available TCP/IP tools.

There are many to try, and we'll cover the four most helpful and common here, including ping, ipconfig, tracert, and netsh. Remember, there are plenty of others, though!

ping

ping is one of the most basic commands in the TC/IP troubleshooting toolkit. It can reveal problems with the host's TCP/IP configuration when used with a local host address. It can also be used to see whether one computer can reach another. It uses echo requests to perform this task and transmits those requests using Internet Control Message Protocol (ICMP).

The syntax is ping followed by the target's name or IP address. You can use this command, like most others, in a command prompt window or a PowerShell window. We'll go old-school and stick with the command prompt.

To see whether your own computer's TC/IP stack is configured properly, combine the ping command with the loopback address of 127.0.0.1. This command sends packets to the local host for testing. If the ping is successful, the local computer's TCP/IP stack is configured properly.

To ping the local host, follow these steps:

1. On the taskbar, type **cmd** and click Command Prompt in the results.

2. Type **ping 127.0.0.1** and press Enter on the keyboard.

3. Note the success or failure in the results. See Figure 3-7.

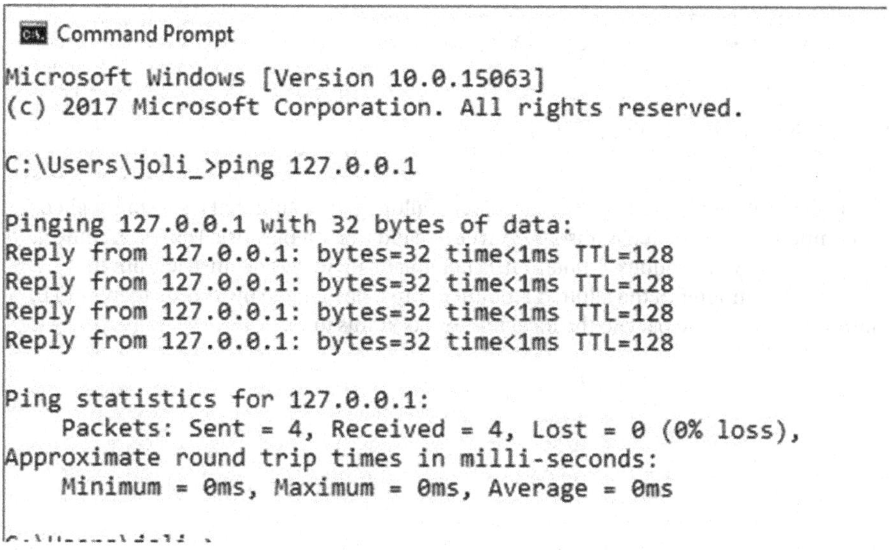

```
Command Prompt
Microsoft Windows [Version 10.0.15063]
(c) 2017 Microsoft Corporation. All rights reserved.

C:\Users\joli_>ping 127.0.0.1

Pinging 127.0.0.1 with 32 bytes of data:
Reply from 127.0.0.1: bytes=32 time<1ms TTL=128
Reply from 127.0.0.1: bytes=32 time<1ms TTL=128
Reply from 127.0.0.1: bytes=32 time<1ms TTL=128
Reply from 127.0.0.1: bytes=32 time<1ms TTL=128

Ping statistics for 127.0.0.1:
    Packets: Sent = 4, Received = 4, Lost = 0 (0% loss),
Approximate round trip times in milli-seconds:
    Minimum = 0ms, Maximum = 0ms, Average = 0ms
```

Figure 3-7. *A successful ping command*

If this command shows a failure (and it will likely show "General failure"), you know something is wrong with the local host's TCP/IP configuration or with the computer itself. Perhaps the proper TCP/IP protocol isn't installed. Other problems could be that the firewall is misconfigured, there are outdated drivers or firmware, there are DNS or socket issues, or there is a general hardware failure.

▪ **Note**   A successful ping to the local host does not mean the network card is working. To see whether the network card is working, ping something outside the computer, such as the default gateway or another computer on the network.

You can also ping another computer. You'll need to know the computer name or IP address first and add it to the command. Figure 3-8 shows a successful ping to a computer on a local network.

```
▨ Command Prompt

C:\Users\joli_>ping hplaptop

Pinging HPLaptop [fe80::35a9:3a5:789:e406%7] with 32 bytes of data:
Reply from fe80::35a9:3a5:789:e406%7: time<1ms
Reply from fe80::35a9:3a5:789:e406%7: time<1ms
Reply from fe80::35a9:3a5:789:e406%7: time<1ms
Reply from fe80::35a9:3a5:789:e406%7: time<1ms

Ping statistics for fe80::35a9:3a5:789:e406%7:
    Packets: Sent = 4, Received = 4, Lost = 0 (0% loss),
Approximate round trip times in milli-seconds:
    Minimum = 0ms, Maximum = 0ms, Average = 0ms
```

Figure 3-8. *A successful ping to a local computer*

Figure 3-9 shows a failure. This particular failure gives a hint that we've misspelled the computer name, which is absolutely true; we did that on purpose. However, some results show that the request "times out." That means there was no answer from the destination computer in the allotted amount of time, designated by its time to live (TTL) value, or that no route back to the local host exists at this time.

■ Command Prompt

```
C:\Users\joli_>ping hplaptop2
Ping request could not find host hplaptop2. Please check the name and try again.

C:\Users\joli_>
```

Figure 3-9. A failed ping to a local computer

The TTL types of failures can be caused for many reasons, but one of the most common is that the remote computer is not turned on. Here are a few others:

- The TTL limit expires for any reason.

- The default gateway can't be reached.

- A firewall is misconfigured.

- There are insufficient network resources.

- There are hardware errors.

- There are router problems.

- The destination host can't receive ping requests.

- There are remote network is unreachable.

If the ping command works, you can move on to other tools, such as ipconfig, tracert, and netsh, detailed next.

ipconfig

ipconfig is another commonly used tool. Like ping, it can be used at a command prompt or in PowerShell. The most common addition to ipconfig is /all, which offers quite a bit of information. Figure 3-10 shows some of the information displayed by ipconfig /all. Note the physical address, that DHCP is enabled, that there are IPv6 and IPv4 addresses assigned, and that the DNS server is set to Google's with an address of 8.8.8.8.

```
Command Prompt

Wireless LAN adapter Wi-Fi:

    Connection-specific DNS Suffix  . : fios-router.home
    Description . . . . . . . . . . . : Intel(R) Dual Band Wireless-AC 7265
    Physical Address. . . . . . . . . : A4-02-B9-6B-0F-62
    DHCP Enabled. . . . . . . . . . . : Yes
    Autoconfiguration Enabled . . . . : Yes
    Link-local IPv6 Address . . . . . : fe80::35a9:3a5:789:e406%7(Preferred)
    IPv4 Address. . . . . . . . . . . : 192.168.1.250(Preferred)
    Subnet Mask . . . . . . . . . . . : 255.255.255.0
    Lease Obtained. . . . . . . . . . : Tuesday, August 8, 2017 8:06:59 AM
    Lease Expires . . . . . . . . . . : Wednesday, August 9, 2017 12:40:13 PM
    Default Gateway . . . . . . . . . : 192.168.1.1
    DHCP Server . . . . . . . . . . . : 192.168.1.1
    DHCPv6 IAID . . . . . . . . . . . : 77857465
    DHCPv6 Client DUID. . . . . . . . : 00-01-00-01-1F-B0-16-5C-EC-8E-B5-48-E6-D3
    DNS Servers . . . . . . . . . . . : 8.8.8.8
                                        8.8.8.4
    NetBIOS over Tcpip. . . . . . . . : Enabled

Ethernet adapter Bluetooth Network Connection:

    Media State . . . . . . . . . . . : Media disconnected
    Connection-specific DNS Suffix  . :
    Description . . . . . . . . . . . : Bluetooth Device (Personal Area Network)
    Physical Address. . . . . . . . . : A4-02-B9-6B-0F-66
    DHCP Enabled. . . . . . . . . . . : Yes
    Autoconfiguration Enabled . . . . : Yes

Tunnel adapter Local Area Connection* 5:

    Connection-specific DNS Suffix  . :
    Description . . . . . . . . . . . : Microsoft Teredo Tunneling Adapter
    Physical Address. . . . . . . . . : 00-00-00-00-00-00-00-E0
    DHCP Enabled. . . . . . . . . . . : No
    Autoconfiguration Enabled . . . . : Yes
    IPv6 Address. . . . . . . . . . . : 2001:0:4137:9e76:141d:3880:3f57:fe05(Preferred)
    Link-local IPv6 Address . . . . . : fe80::141d:3880:3f57:fe05%10(Preferred)
    Default Gateway . . . . . . . . . : ::
    DHCPv6 IAID . . . . . . . . . . . : 167772160
    DHCPv6 Client DUID. . . . . . . . : 00-01-00-01-1F-B0-16-5C-EC-8E-B5-48-E6-D3
    NetBIOS over Tcpip. . . . . . . . : Disabled
```

Figure 3-10. *Results of the ipconfig /all command*

The information offered makes it easy to see whether DHCP is the problem, for instance, by whether the lease is active or not. Beyond what's shown in Figure 3-10, though, you can also learn the following:

- The host name

- Which network adapter is active if more than one exists

- If Bluetooth is active, enabled, and/or connected

- How tunneling is configured, if it is

With this information at hand, you can begin the troubleshooting process. For instance, if you learn DHCP is disabled, it's easy enough to enable it!

tracert

If packets are lost along the way from the host to destination computer, you can figure out where by using the tracert command. It's easier than trying to ping each router along a path that packets can take and likely impossible anyway since multiple paths exist. It works like the ping command does, by sending ICMP echo requests, but modifies the TTL values as those messages move from router to router so that the request won't time out. In doing so, it's possible to see where packets get held up or fail in their transmission.

To use tracert, simply type tracert followed by the destination computer. Figure 3-11 shows the results of tracert www.wellbeingstx.com.

```
🖥 Command Prompt

C:\Users\joli_>tracert www.wellbeingstx.com

Tracing route to wellbeingstx.com [72.167.191.69]
over a maximum of 30 hops:

  1     3 ms    <1 ms    <1 ms  192.168.1.1
  2     9 ms    10 ms    10 ms  47.184.128.1
  3    11 ms    12 ms     9 ms  172.102.50.212
  4    14 ms    11 ms    10 ms  ae8---0.scr02.dlls.tx.frontiernet.net [74.40.3.25]
  5    11 ms    12 ms    21 ms  ae1---0.cbr01.dlls.tx.frontiernet.net [74.40.1.82]
  6     *        *        *     Request timed out.
  7     *        *        *     Request timed out.
  8    33 ms    32 ms    36 ms  4.28.83.74
  9    34 ms    31 ms    36 ms  be38.trmc0215-01.ars.mgmt.phx3.gdg [184.168.0.69]
 10    32 ms    35 ms    33 ms  be38.trmc0215-01.ars.mgmt.phx3.gdg [184.168.0.69]
 11    34 ms    33 ms    34 ms  ip-97-74-255-129.ip.secureserver.net [97.74.255.129]
 12    32 ms    33 ms    34 ms  ip-72-167-191-69.ip.secureserver.net [72.167.191.69]

Trace complete.
```

Figure 3-11. *A successful traceroute command*

You can use the information here to see where a failure occurs. If any of these routers are on the enterprise network, those routers can be examined, for instance.

netsh

netsh enables you to review information about the networks you can access, but it is also a scripting tool. Using scripts and applicable commands, you can modify the network configuration. You learned a little about netsh in Chapter 2. You run netsh from a command line to start that process.

There are hundreds of commands you can use with netsh. With regard to this chapter, though, specifically with your introduction about the OSI model and the various layers, we'll introduce the netsh reset command. The reset parameter lets you repair the TCP/IP stack on a local computer. In doing so, you can automatically fix any issues between the OSI layers that have become misaligned or otherwise broken. You will want to run this command if you can ping a host but you can't connect to your network or the Internet, for instance. Of course, there are other reasons, but this is one that is most easily understood.

The reset command for Windows 10 is netsh int ip reset resetlog.txt. Use this at an elevated command prompt. Once you run the command, you'll immediately see the results of the fix. You'll need to restart the computer to apply any changes. Figure 3-12 shows that everything is well here, at least for now.

```
▨ Administrator: Command Prompt
Microsoft Windows [Version 10.0.15063]
(c) 2017 Microsoft Corporation. All rights reserved.

C:\WINDOWS\system32>netsh int ip reset resetlog.txt
Resetting Compartment Forwarding, OK!
Resetting Compartment, OK!
Resetting Control Protocol, OK!
Resetting Echo Sequence Request, OK!
Resetting Global, OK!
Resetting Interface, OK!
Resetting Anycast Address, OK!
Resetting Multicast Address, OK!
Resetting Unicast Address, OK!
Resetting Neighbor, OK!
Resetting Path, OK!
Resetting Potential, OK!
Resetting Prefix Policy, OK!
Resetting Proxy Neighbor, OK!
Resetting Route, OK!
Resetting Site Prefix, OK!
Resetting Subinterface, OK!
Resetting Wakeup Pattern, OK!
Resetting Resolve Neighbor, OK!
Resetting , OK!
Resetting , OK!
Resetting , OK!
Resetting , OK!
Resetting , failed.
Access is denied.

Resetting , OK!
Resetting , OK!
Resetting , OK!
Resetting , OK!
Resetting , OK!
Resetting , OK!
Resetting , OK!
Restart the computer to complete this action.
```

Figure 3-12. Using the netsh reset command

netsh works in many other ways. Type **netsh** at the command prompt and press Enter on the keyboard and you'll see that the prompt changes from C>\Users\username to netsh>. From here you can apply netsh commands to specific protocols and technology including DHCP, routing, WINS, and more. For example, while inside the netsh environment, you can enter the DHCP environment by typing **DHCP** and pressing Enter. From there you can add and delete DHCP servers, among other things. However, we're not here to teach you this; we're here to help you fix issues with TCP/IP and, specifically, the TCP/IP stack.

Summary

The main purpose of a network is to securely connect computers and users for the purpose of sharing resources and doing work. When networks consist of varying infrastructure, such as Apple and Windows devices, wired and wireless devices, and desktop and mobile workstations, like almost all networks do, it's imperative they all communicate seamlessly. To do this, all must agree on specific rules called *protocols*, and the OSI model outlines these for manufacturers and administrators around the world. Of course, when problems arise, and they do, there are tools available to help. Common tools include ping, ipconfig, tracert, and netsh, but others exist.

CHAPTER 4

■ ■ ■

What Causes Networking Problems

There's a tendency for people to think of a computer as an isolated, stand-alone machine. In reality, because of our network and Internet connections, no computer is isolated. Everything is connected to everything else, and your Internet connection allows your computer to connect to, and be connected to from, just about any other computer on Earth.

When it comes to the Internet, the mentality is one that often affects motorists, where they think of themselves as separated from the world outside their vehicle by a metal cage. Likewise, people consider the Internet as just being something on their device that allows them to send messages to friends and do some shopping in complete isolation to everybody else.

In reality, the truth is extremely different. If you take a look around your home right now, you can probably list a huge number of devices that are connected both to the Internet and to each other. This list could include tablets, laptops, desktop PCs, Xbox consoles, smartphones, Amazon Echo devices, routers, printers, IP video cameras, networked-attached storage (NAS) appliances, televisions, and maybe even a smart mattress cover on your bed.

You may additionally have a smartwatch and Internet of Things (IoT) devices such as smart lighting or heating, an Internet-connected refrigerator (if you're one of the three people who ever purchased one), maybe a smart bathroom mirror, and perhaps even a drone or a robot.

If you look then to the average workplace, there will be network switches, more network storage, perhaps a server or two, more IP cameras and security systems, additional printers and scanners, and visitor devices attaching to the Wi-Fi network.

All of this is connected, through the router, to cloud datacenters that provide access to Office 365, e-mail, Dropbox, Amazon S3 and Google storage, and web and remote intranet sites across your own country and the rest of the world.

These connections are made through vast networks of cellular masts and telephone exchanges and datacenters run by your ISP (and in the case of some countries, managed and regulated by the government of that country itself).

The whole interconnectedness of things means that every device on Earth is, theoretically at least, connected simultaneously to every other device on Earth. It's because of this interconnectedness that criminals are able to control vast armies of bots—malware-infected PCs that can be used to bring down the web sites and networks

© Mike Halsey and Joli Ballew 2017
M. Halsey and J. Ballew, *Windows Networking Troubleshooting*,
https://doi.org/10.1007/978-1-4842-3222-4_4

of major corporations. It's also because of this interconnectedness that our computing devices have firewalls, antivirus software, and end-user security in place. Additionally, because of this interconnectedness of things, sharing a funny photo of your dogs is now significantly simpler than printing 20 copies of it on glossy photo paper and buying a book of stamps and some envelopes.

The biggest threat to our PCs and networks, however, isn't criminals, hackers, or even poorly written code. No, by far the biggest threat to our PCs and networks are the people who need to use them. It's often said that a PC that's left in the box and never plugged into an electricity socket will never go wrong. This might come from the amusing anecdote school of thought, but it's also very accurate. Those who most want to use computers are, by their very definition, those who should least be allowed to do so.

You might argue then that it's the responsibility of the software, hardware, and operating system (OS) vendors to ensure that their systems are safe to use and robust and that they ensure there are never any bugs or problems with the code (and hardware) that they release.

This brings us to Microsoft Windows. This operating system has three critical flaws when it comes to preventing problems from occurring. The first is that this venerable operating system is required by far too many of its users (including ourselves) to be backward compatible with software and hardware that predates the World Wide Web, sometimes by some decades. The second is that it needs to run and be compatible with tens of thousands of new hardware devices and software apps every year, on a regular basis and immediately upon their release. Lastly, the Windows OS itself consists of millions of lines of code, and there's not one person on Earth who could ever single-handedly keep track of it all.

With all this in mind, it's frankly amazing that Microsoft ever manages to make its operating systems stable and reliable at all. Indeed, we've been many times to the main building on Microsoft's campus in Redmond, Washington, where it's developed (see Figure 4-1), and it's a surprisingly ordinary and unassuming office block, populated entirely by equally surprisingly ordinary men and women who are all just like us. This makes them fallible and prone to all the attention and productivity problems that face the rest of us first thing on a Monday morning (or indeed on any morning).

Figure 4-1. Building 37 on the Microsoft campus in Redmond

The Leg Bone's Connected to the...

You've probably heard the "Dem Bones" (sometimes called "Dry Bones") song about how the bones in the human body are connected to one another. It's important to remember that all our computing devices are interconnected in a similar manner.

You might, for example, find that you have no network connection on a PC but there appears to be nothing wrong with the driver. In this circumstance, you need to look at everything else that sits in the chain between the PC and the network or Internet.

This includes cabling, both from the PC to the network socket (and the socket itself) and from that socket to the switch or router. It doesn't stop there either as you then have the router and switch hardware, the communications box on your street, the ISP, and maybe even the electric company digging a trench on the building site next door.

A good place to start with any type of network problem is to first ask if anybody else, or any other device, is also experiencing a problem. This can quickly help you determine whether the problem is specific to that one PC or caused by something external to the PC.

If other people or other devices are also experiencing a problem, then it's clear troubleshooting one device isn't going to help, at least not unless it's a PC causing the problem (such as a greedy downloader app chewing all the Internet bandwidth).

Looking at networking problems holistically then is essential and comes down to the three basic tenets of troubleshooting network problems.

- Is the problem isolated to one device, or are other devices also experiencing an issue?

- Has something changed recently on that PC or elsewhere on the network?

- Is this a recurrence of a problem that has appeared before, either on this or on another device?

Common Network Problems

Having established that computing devices are a melting pot of problems, all of which are just waiting to happen, let's spend some time looking at the most common problems and how they afflict our PCs and networks.

These common problems fall into a variety of categories that are caused by human error, OS problems, software issues, and hardware incompatibilities.

We'd like to begin this by saying that by far the most useful networking tool any IT professional or systems administrator can keep in their arsenal is a USB-to-Ethernet adapter dongle, as shown in Figure 4-2. You will probably also want a variety of USB plug adapters so that you can ensure this dongle will work with all the many types of USB port you'll find on devices.

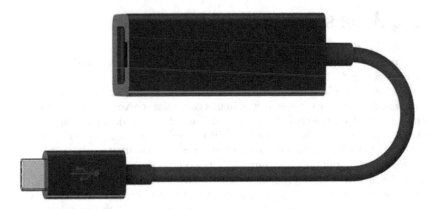

Figure 4-2. A USB/Ethernet dongle adapter

Wi-Fi Driver Issues

The venerable Ethernet cabling system, which has connected PCs together and allowed them fast and reliable access to the Internet, is fast becoming redundant. Long gone are the days when Wi-Fi and other wireless networking technologies were slow and had limited bandwidth capacity. As I write this, the latest Wi-Fi standard, 802.11ax, is being prepped for launch. This new specification will permit wireless data connections up to 10 gigabits per second (Gbps), with 1Gb being 125MB). That might still sound slow compared to the 100Gbps available with fast Ethernet connections, but just look at how quickly the technology has developed.

In February 2015, researchers at the University of Surrey (UK) achieved a speed of 1 terabit per second (Tbps), or 125GB, over the new 5G data network. This connection is considerably faster than the fastest Ethernet commercially available (at 12.5GB), and while new Ethernet standards up to 800Gbps are under development, it's unlikely that anybody will want to further refine wired data connections in the future.

For this reason, our top networking problem—Wi-Fi driver issues—usually requires you have an Ethernet dongle in hand. This technology might be about to be superseded by faster wireless standards, but it'll still be useful and likely found on routers for many years to come.

There are several causes of Wi-Fi driver issues, defined by a problem that prevents the driver from being unable to connect the PC to a wireless network.

- *Driver updates* are by far the most common cause of broken Wi-Fi connections. This includes both automatic updates (delivered through either Windows Update or a vendor's own driver update app) and drivers that are manually updated by the user. We'll show you how to manage drivers later in this chapter.

- *Fresh OS installs* can also break Wi-Fi connectivity. Performing a clean installation of Windows on a laptop or tablet (i.e., any device that's not connected to the router via Ethernet) can result in the Windows installer not having or finding the correct Wi-Fi driver. In this circumstance, the PC then cannot get online to download the correct driver, and it will need to be connected via Ethernet or have the driver manually downloaded on another PC and transferred by a USB flash drive.

- *Disconnected/broken antennas* are another but far less common issue. This can affect both external and internal antennas.

- *Software/hardware conflicts* are another uncommon cause of problems. However, some PCs come with vendor-produced management apps for Wi-Fi. These apps could become corrupt or develop a fault of some kind. Additionally, it's rare that Windows versions will encounter hardware conflicts, but assuming nothing will ever happen is probably foolhardy.

- *Signal issues* are the next common cause of Wi-Fi connection problems. It might seem daft to ask a user to walk with their device into the next room or closer to the router to see whether they get their connection back, but you'd be surprised how often dead spots in buildings can be found. This is something we'll talk about later in this chapter.

- Lastly, *connecting to the wrong Wi-Fi network* is something that happens with such alarming regularity that it might be enough to make you cry with laughter.

Misconfigured Network Settings

Another common cause of network connection problems is misconfigured settings. This can be both in the driver and in the Wi-Fi authentication settings. In the next chapter, we'll show you how to reset the TCP/IP networking stack on a PC, but you can also sometimes find that the settings that allow a PC to connect to a specific network have become corrupt.

If this happens, you will need to manually delete the Wi-Fi connection profile for that network and then reconnect from scratch (for which you will then need the password). The way you do this varies in Windows versions.

Deleting Network Profiles in Windows 7

To manually delete a Wi-Fi network profile in Windows 7, follow these instructions:

1. Open the Network and Sharing Center from the Control Panel.

2. In the left pane, click Manage Wireless Networks.

3. Right-click the network you want to delete and then click "Remove network" from the menu that appears.

Deleting Network Profiles in Windows 8.1

With Windows 8.1, the process to delete Wi-Fi network profiles is very different.

1. Open the Settings app and navigate to the Network panel.

2. In the Connections section, click the "Manage known connections" link in the Wi-Fi section.

3. Click the network you want to delete and then click the Forget button that appears.

Deleting Network Profiles in Windows 10

You probably won't be surprised to hear at this point that the way you delete Wi-Fi network profiles in Windows 10 is, again, different, though not by much.

1. Open Settings and then the Network & Internet panel.

2. In the Wi-Fi section, click the "Manage known networks" link in the Wi-Fi section.

3. Click the network you want to delete and then click the Forget button that appears.

Deleting Network Profiles from the Command Line

It's also possible in every version of Windows to delete network profiles from a command prompt (with administrator privileges). To do this, use the following commands:

1. Type **netsh wlan show profiles** to display a list of all the known Wi-Fi networks the PC connects to, as shown in Figure 4-3.

```
■ Administrator Command Prompt                                        –  □  ×
(c) 2015 Microsoft Corporation. All rights reserved.

C:\WINDOWS\system32>netsh wlan show profiles

Profiles on interface Wi-Fi:

Group policy profiles (read only)
---------------------------------
    <None>

User profiles
-------------
    All User Profile     : Plusnetwireless707D73
    All User Profile     : virginmedia7224139
    All User Profile     : Lumia 950 4322
    All User Profile     : 6 Pax
    All User Profile     : Princess
    All User Profile     : mvp2015
    All User Profile     : 6 Pax
    All User Profile     : AIR-2602I
    All User Profile     : 6 Pax+
    All User Profile     : EE-BrightBox-htndfh
    All User Profile     : NOKIA 909_0845
    All User Profile     : ZyXEL_A39C
    All User Profile     : NOKIA 909_9800
    All User Profile     : MMU-Visitor
    All User Profile     : BTHub3-2CSW

C:\WINDOWS\system32>
```

Figure 4-3. You can delete Wi-Fi profiles from the command line

2. Type **netsh wlan delete profile name=**"*network name*" to delete the appropriate profile.

■ **Tip** If you don't know the password for a Wi-Fi network so that you can reconnect to it or if you just want to know a Wi-Fi network access password so that you can use it on another PC, use the command `netsh wlan show profiles name="network name" key=clear` to display full details about the network. The access password will appear in the Key content field.

Hardware Issues

A variety of hardware issues can negatively impact on network performance or availability. Keeping cables tidy, manageable, and out of the way of users is always a good idea. Snagged cables, where a user accidentally pulls or trips one, are commonplace and can cause more damage sometimes that just a broken plug.

Damage to network sockets can be caused, often requiring expensive motherboard replacements, excessive downtime, and perhaps even injury to the person who snagged the cable.

Placing network hardware in inappropriate locations can also cause network issues. Excessively hot, cold, or dusty environments will cause damage to any appliance over time.

Additionally, you should be aware of what can happen to mobile hardware. You may be the sort of person who takes extremely good care of your hardware and devices. This can help them have a good, long life span and even look almost new when they are eventually retired.

Many people, however, do not treat technology respectfully. They'll throw it around, drop it carelessly, give it to young children and teenagers who will do everything from banging it to trying to suck on it,[1] and more besides.

User Error

Returning to what we said earlier about a PC that's never used never having a problem, you'd be amazed just how much users who shouldn't, or who perhaps shouldn't even be able to, change settings and configurations on a PC actually do so.

To be honest, this is part of the point of asking the question "What's changed?" It's entirely possible that a networking issue has arisen because of a recent driver or Windows update. It's fairly likely, though, that a problem has occurred because a user was trying to effect a change of their own on the PC that they shouldn't have done.

This could be something as straightforward as connecting their PC to a different Wi-Fi network so as to get a better signal. Their Internet connection might now be great, but all of a sudden, they'll find their network storage access is unavailable.

---

[1] If you have the image of a teenager trying to suck on a laptop stuck in your mind at this point, you're not alone.

Unless the settings on a PC are locked down in Group Policy, all manner of changes can be made. This can cause particular issues with BYOD devices, where a user be will their own administrator. Here you don't have the permissions you require to lock absolutely everything down. Thus, asking the "What's changed?" question and pressing the user to be honest about what they might have done can save considerable amounts of diagnostic and repair time, not to mention wasted engineer site visits.

Updates and Patches

Updates and patches for PCs fall into two distinct categories: those that come directly from Microsoft via Windows Update and those that come from third-party vendors. The former is something you can get significant amounts of control over through Windows Server Update Services (WSUS) and Update Branches (available in Windows 10). The latter will come through installed vendor utilities, and they are much harder to control.

As an example, when you install a driver for a piece of Wi-Fi networking hardware, you will sometimes find the vendor includes its own Wi-Fi connection and management utility, which will autorun when Windows starts and essentially hijack the entire connection process.

Should your business use a Wi-Fi network with specialist settings, especially custom security settings, you'll often find that such a utility will play havoc with connections. Disabling these utilities is sometimes not enough because if the vendor has placed an updater app in the background, you may find that the very tool you have disabled comes back into foreground use a few months later.

Taming Windows Update

We're very much from the "if it ain't broke, don't fix it" school. While this is generally a good rule in life, it's not often a good rule when it comes to PC security and stability. A stable network driver might not always be a secure network driver. This isn't going to be because it won't connect to your networks securely (though anything is possible), but there could be coding or security vulnerabilities in the driver itself that permits malware or hackers to gain backdoor access to the PC.

If you work in an enterprise environment, where you have a volume license subscription from Microsoft, then you'll likely already be using Windows Software Update Services (WSUS) to manage updates. This allows you to test and evaluate drivers and other updates before deploying them to see that they're stable and won't cause issues with the unique combinations of hardware and software that you use.

Outside of a WSUS environment, however, it's not so easy. An SMB might have several dozen stand-alone machines. They're probably all either identical or very similar to one another. This means an incompatible driver download can render almost every machine unusable.

While this situation is unlikely, it's possible to prevent Windows from automatically updating the drivers on your PCs.

Preventing Driver Updates in Windows 7 and 8.1

To disable driver updates in Windows, open the System panel from the Control Panel and then click the Advanced System Settings link in the left pane.

This will display the System Properties dialog, as shown in Figure 4-4. Click the Hardware tab and then the Device Installation Settings button to display the driver installation options.

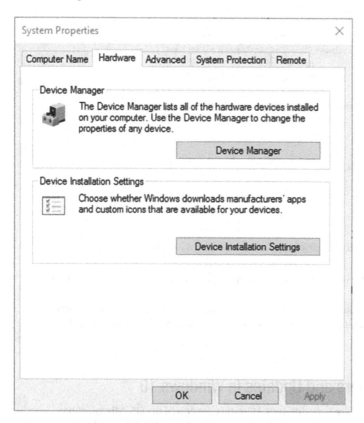

Figure 4-4. You can disable driver updates in Windows

What you see next will depend on which version of Windows you're using. In Windows 7, as shown in Figure 4-5, you have the options "Always install the best driver...," "Install from Windows Update if the driver is not found on my computer," and "Never install driver software from Windows Update."

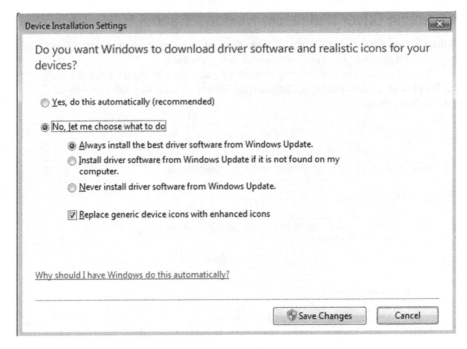

Figure 4-5. *You can disable driver updates in Windows 7 and 8.1*

In Windows 8.1, you'll see the options "Always install drivers" and "Never install drivers."

Bear in mind, though, that disabling this feature in either OS will also prevent Windows from searching for the correct driver when you plug in or install a new piece of hardware on the PC.

Managing Drivers and Updates in Windows 10

In Windows 10 things are very different. With this version of the OS, Microsoft has changed the policies governing completely opt out and mandated that nobody, no matter who they are, can opt out of downloading and installing security and stability updates.

If you open Device Installation Settings from the Windows 10 System panel, you will only see options to block a manufacturer's apps and custom icons, as shown in Figure 4-6.

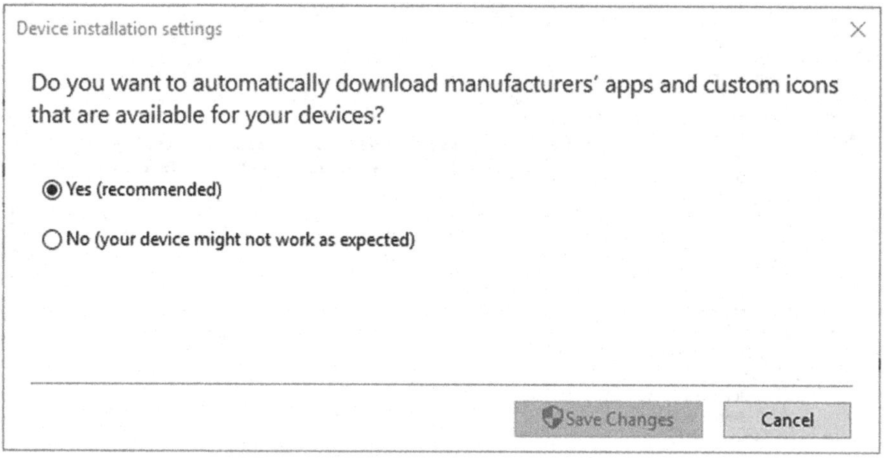

Device installation settings ✕

Do you want to automatically download manufacturers' apps and custom icons that are available for your devices?

◉ Yes (recommended)

○ No (your device might not work as expected)

⏷ Save Changes | Cancel

Figure 4-6. *You cannot block driver updates from the Windows 10 Control Panel*

Admittedly, this is still a useful setting to use in some circumstances because it will block the auto-updating of Wi-Fi management software like the kind we mentioned earlier.

■ **Note**   Windows 10 Pro and Enterprise users have two additional, advanced options for Windows updates. Both editions have the option "Defer feature updates," which will delay the downloading of new OS features for up to three months; this feature is called Current Branch for Business (CBB). Enterprise editions also have a feature called Long Term Servicing Branch (LTSB), which will delay feature updates for a period of up to ten years. Neither of these branches, however, will delay security, stability, or driver updates.

Managing Driver Install Notifications in Group Policy

Driver updates and downloads can also be managed using Group Policy in Windows Pro and Enterprise editions. To access this, search for *gpedit* (sometimes *gpedit.msc*) at the Start menu, where you will probably need to right-click and run the Group Policy Editor as an administrator.

Navigate to Administrative Templates ➤ System ➤ Driver Installation, and you will see the option "Turn off Windows Update device driver search prompt," as shown in Figure 4-7.

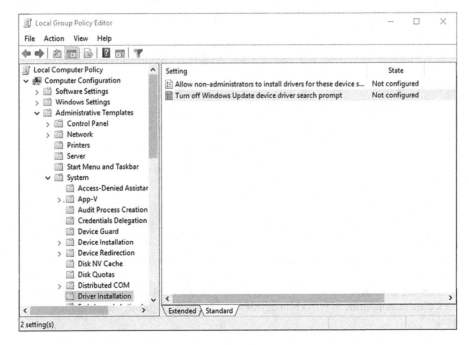

Figure 4-7. You can manage driver downloads in Group Policy

Enabling this setting *will not* disable driver downloads, but it will prevent dialog messages from prompting users to automatically check Windows Update for a new or updated driver. This can help prevent users from installing driver updates that can cause problems or incompatibilities on the PC.

Drivers and Hardware

Once a driver is installed, there are various ways in which you can manage it, all of which are done through Device Manager (available in the Control Panel or via a search). Device Manager contains a great many useful tools for solving problems with both hardware and software devices on the PC.

At its most basic, double-clicking a device will display a dialog containing everything you need to know about it, as shown in Figure 4-8, from whether it's working correctly to the driver version number (useful in making sure you have the latest one or one that's known to be free of bugs and problems) to advanced information about the driver properties.

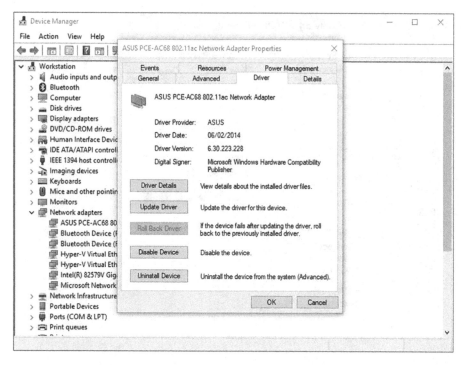

Figure 4-8. *Useful tools and information exist within Device Manager*

Obtaining Advanced Driver Information

The Advanced and Details tabs in the properties dialog contain a huge amount of extremely useful information and configuration options.

The Advanced tab, for example, provides configuration options for the network adapter that might need configuration to get the adapter working correctly with some secure network types. The exact options that you see, as shown in Figure 4-9, will vary depending on the exact adapter and adapter type you have installed, but you can see in the example that a great many different configuration options exist.

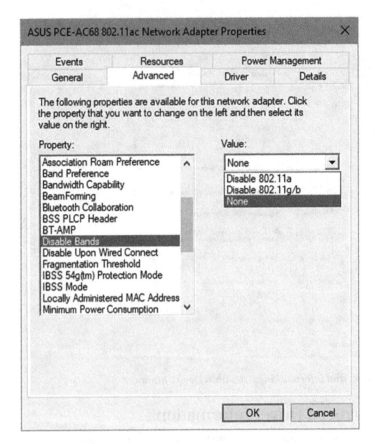

Figure 4-9. *You can configure advanced network adapter properties*

When it comes to configuring these options, what you need to check and change will be very specific to the needs of your local network and its security settings, so you should check with the specifications and requirements of the network before making any changes.

If you need to get information about the network adapter, you can do this on the Details tab, as shown in Figure 4-10. You will see that a drop-down menu contains a wealth of different options that can give you detailed information about the network adapter. Selecting an option will display the relevant information in a panel below the drop-down options box.

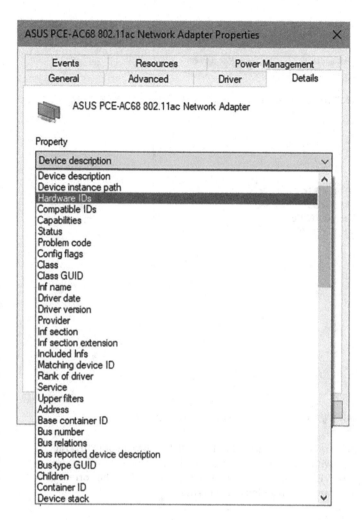

Figure 4-10. *The Details tab provides advanced information about the network adapter*

Identifying Unknown Drivers

It's on the Details tab where you can find the information needed to identify hardware devices that are displaying in Device Manager as "Unknown." Figure 4-11 shows that we have selected the Hardware IDs option from the Details tab. This displays the VEN_ (Vendor) and DEV_ (Device) codes for the device, in this case being VEN_14E4 and DEV_43A0.

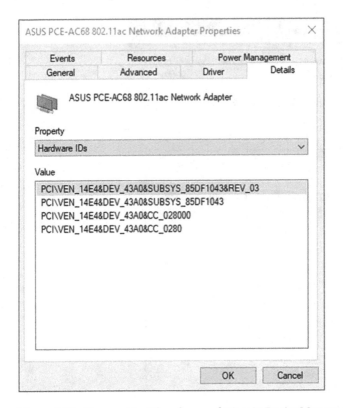

Figure 4-11. *You can identify unknown devices in Device Manager*

A quick search online reveals this particular device to be a Broadcom 802.11ac Network Adapter chipset, with some links online correctly identifying it further as an ASUS device. By using the VEN_ and DEV_ codes, you can quickly find the correct drivers for the device so that you can get it installed and working.

Getting Information About Driver Errors

The Events tab in the driver's Properties dialog is a useful way to find out about any errors or problems that have arisen with a specific driver. It will detail the time, date, and description of any recent errors or problems. There is also a View All Events button that launches the Event Manager and can give you much more advanced information about the driver, including all errors and events associated with it, as shown in Figure 4-12.

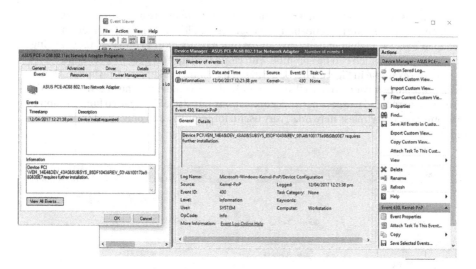

Figure 4-12. Device Manager hooks into the Event Viewer

The Event Viewer displays advanced information for every event, which can include error codes, in the format 0x000..., that you can search for online to get further information. However, the information in the Event Viewer goes further, detailing the user who was signed into the PC when the event occurred and more besides.

You can attach an event to an error if you want by highlighting the error in the Event Viewer and then clicking the Attach Task To This Event link that appears near the bottom-right corner of the Event Viewer window. When you attach a task to an event, you have the choice of starting a program (such as diagnostic or test utility for the device), sending an e-mail (an e-mail client on the PC isn't required; you just need a valid SMTP address), or displaying a message. The latter can be useful if you need a user to immediately stop whatever they're doing so that they can call a support person and describe to them exactly what was happening at the time, such as what apps they were using.

Software Problems and Incompatibilities

On a related note to hardware drivers is software. It's common, especially with Wi-Fi hardware, for vendors to install their own connection and management utilities on PCs as part of the driver installation, and these can frequently cause problems.

As an example, over the years we've seen Wi-Fi drivers completely unable to connect to certain network types, especially secure networks, because the utility software wasn't capable of connecting to, or reliably connecting to, that type of network.

In fairness, we've never (not since Windows XP anyway) seen an example where uninstalling the software utility caused the driver to become unresponsive and unable to connect to any network. The Wi-Fi connection subsystem in modern Windows versions is extremely robust and reliable.

When it comes to the chances of other, third-party software and apps causing problems with a network connection, the chances are slim to none unless that software is set up in a way as to deliberately consume as much bandwidth as possible, thus slowing the connection, which can be common with cloud backup and peer-to-peer apps.

In the example in Figure 4-13, you can see the cloud backup app Crashplan. This is an example of an app done well as it not only allows you to limit the bandwidth used over both wired and wireless network connections but also allows you to limit the app to use only specific wireless networks (very useful for security) and only specific network adapters.

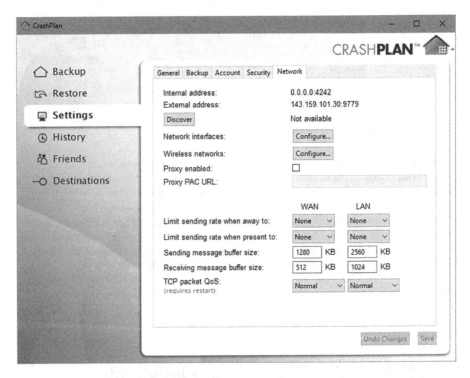

Figure 4-13. Many apps have network configuration options

If you use cloud or peer-to-peer backup and file sync apps in your business or organization, it's well worth checking the software provided by the vendor in advance to see whether these types of options are provided or supported.

Wi-Fi Interference

If you're living in Wisconsin and are reading this, then yippee! If you're reading this in Rome, then boo-hoo! What do we mean by this? Quite simply, the biggest barrier to having a stable Wi-Fi connection is the quality and materials the building you're in is made from.

In countries such as the United States and Canada, houses are commonly made from wood and are usually no more than 60 or 70 years old. Elsewhere in the world, you could find yourself in a building that's hundreds or even thousands of years old and where the walls are made from a thick stone construction.

Nothing will block a Wi-Fi signal more effectively than a thick brick or stone wall (useful information to pass on to anybody who might like wearing a tinfoil hat).

There are various solutions you can employ to mitigate this problem, with perhaps the most obvious being installation of a wired network. However, not all mobile devices come with an Ethernet port; in fact, it's uncommon these days to find one on an ultrabook, and when it comes to tablets, you can forget having an Ethernet port without using a USB dongle to give you one.

The best example of boosting a Wi-Fi signal in this type of circumstance is through using a mesh network. Mesh networks use a series of routers placed around a building, connected either through Ethernet or wirelessly, to create a more even Wi-Fi signal throughout the premises. This is similar to the process of setting up Wi-Fi repeaters, though in the case of a mesh network, the devices are intended to be used together, and they will often use the close (technical) bond they have to aid you in placing them in the optimum locations (usually through use of a mobile app) to get the best signal.

Network Hardware Problems

When it comes to networks where you're not connecting, or not connecting all your machines, through Wi-Fi, there can still be bottlenecks and problems caused. This is commonly through the three different types of hardware device you'll find on a network: the switch, the router, and the firewall/security appliance.

For a device with absolutely zero moving parts, we've frequently been amazed just how unreliable and prone to breakage network switches can be. Fortunately, diagnosis of a faulty network switch is usually fairly straightforward, as it's very unlikely a single PC will be affected. It's much more likely that a bank of ports on the switch, or the entire switch, will fail.

Routers present problems too, and it's important not to get a cheap one. When you're investing in a router, you should consider what advanced functionality the router will offer. Is it part of an expandable mesh system, and how many different Wi-Fi SSIDs will it offer? The latter is likely the most important consideration as it allows you to isolate parts of your network so that you can, for example, give BYOD and guest devices access to the Internet, and perhaps a joint file or printer share, while keeping them isolated from all the private and important shares.

Firewall and security appliances can often cause problems, and this normally occurs when they are updated in software or firmware. If you have, as an example, a net filtering appliance that can automatically prevent access to gambling or other web sites you'd prefer people to not visit, your built-in whitelists of permitted sites can sometimes be wiped in an update. Thus, it's always best to keep a backup copy of those whitelists, and blacklists, as recovering after a problem can take many hours of tedious work.

Summary

There are a great many different things that can cause problems with network connections on PC, and they range from driver problems all the way down to the physical structure of a building. It gets even worse when you start considering any environmental or third-party factors. Thus, it's always a good idea to ask, "Is this happening to anyone else?" A network problem that's being experienced on more than one PC cannot be isolated to that PC, and thus asking questions such as this can help determine the difference between a driver problem and a digger on the building site next door having just ripped up the fiber cable.

Dealing with these issues is another matter entirely, though, and that's what we'll cover in the next chapter, when you examine in detail how to troubleshoot and repair problems with network hardware and the Windows networking subsystem.

CHAPTER 5

■ ■ ■

Troubleshooting Networking

The methods and tools that you'll use to repair networking problems in Windows vary in use and complexity depending on the task at hand. As an example, some tools are completely automated, needing just a click to go off and do their job, while others require delving into complex administrative utilities or even the Windows command prompt.

It's true then that troubleshooting and repairing networking problems on PCs can be highly complex, especially once you take into account all of the external factors that could also be the cause of problems. In this chapter, though, we'll guide you through the methods you'll use to repair many different types of networking issues.

Managing Routers

Routers are the gateways to the wider world, so it's important that they're correctly managed. This is both for reasons of maintaining stable and reliable Internet and network connections and for maintaining high levels of security on your network and PCs. Remember that the security on PCs and networks is only ever as good as its weakest component.

Good and proper management of routers is pretty much just best practice, and by following a few simple rules, you can ensure that your router is safe and secure and that it will provide high levels of service throughout its life.

- Always change both the default password on the router and the administrator username to something secure. It's all too easy for people to look up the defaults on the Internet.

- Configure one or more guest Wi-Fi networks for visitors to your premises that do not have access to file shares, printers, and servers on the network or that only have access to noncritical file shares and accessible printers.

- If the router supports it, configure bandwidth management on specific Wi-Fi networks to prevent individual users or malware from slowing down the network.

- If you have any mission-critical systems, connect them to a router that also supports 4G or 5G backup connectivity, but do not permit the rest of the business to use this expensive connection medium.

© Mike Halsey and Joli Ballew 2017
M. Halsey and J. Ballew, *Windows Networking Troubleshooting*,
https://doi.org/10.1007/978-1-4842-3222-4_5

- Always connect your PCs, but especially your primary network and Internet connection equipment, to surge protectors, as storms can quickly fry any hardware connected to the outside world via a cable.

- If possible, connect your files shares and critical network infrastructure to two different networks, where the primary one that's accessible to all PCs on the network can be easily and quickly disabled in the event of a malware or hacking attack. This will leave your critical systems still able to function.

The Windows Automated Troubleshooters

Windows comes with automated troubleshooters that can be accessed through the Troubleshooting section of the Control Panel. These are cmdlets that will just reset specific components to their default states. This is literally all that the troubleshooters do, but they can be useful in some circumstances.

The networking troubleshooters contain utilities that can reset Internet connections, file shares, network adapters, and more, as shown in Figure 5-1. You can find more troubleshooters online through the Microsoft Support web site (`https://support.microsoft.com`) by searching for specific problem types.

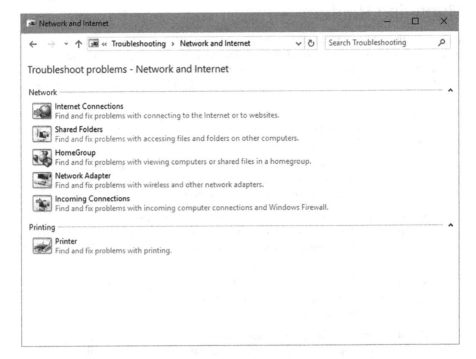

Figure 5-1. *Automated troubleshooters can repair some types of networking issues*

You can also create your own custom automated troubleshooters, perhaps to easily fix common problems with specific hardware in your company. The documentation for this was created for Windows 7 and is online at http://pcs.tv/2vX5YqB.

System Restore

Many IT professionals shy away from using System Restore because back in the days of Windows XP, when it was first introduced, malware would often hide there, waiting to be restored after you thought you'd cleaned it.

With the advent of User Account Control (UAC) in Vista, that all changed, and with Windows 7 and later, security was beefed up even further to prevent malware from infecting the System Restore archive.

System Restore uses the System Volume Information folders you might have seen in the root of each drive on a PC, and when an action occurs in which something changes, such as installing or removing an app or driver or installing a Windows Update, a snapshot of all the critical files and files that are affected by the process is taken. This includes making a backup copy of the Windows Registry.

You configure System Restore from the System controls in the Control Panel, by clicking the "System protection" link in its top-right corner. Perhaps, though, the quickest way is to search for sysdm.cpl in the Start menu.

System Restore can be configured for each drive individually, and while it can be used to cache older copies of files when they are changed, in reality this feature is being deprecated in Windows as it's never truly worked reliably. Thus, the only drives you really need to have System Restore configured for are your Windows drive and any others on which you installed software.

Clicking the Configure button in the System Protection section of the System Properties panel will enable you to turn System Restore on or off for the selected disk and to choose how much space on the disk is devoted to System Restore, as shown in Figure 5-2.

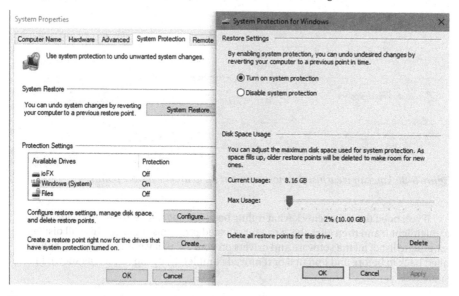

Figure 5-2. *System Restore can be configured from the Control Panel*

Remember that the amount of space you allocate will directly determine how many restore points are kept on the machine. If you have a machine with regular installs and updates being applied, you might want to allocate more space than the default.

If you do suspect that malware has somehow wormed its way into System Restore, there is a Delete button that will remove all the contents of the System Volume Information folder for that drive.

Back in the main System Protection panel, you can manually create a restore point should you want, perhaps because you're taking an action on the PC where you're unsure if System Restore will operate automatically, and you want to be able to roll back your changes should something go wrong.

If you need to restore Windows to an earlier point, click the System Restore button to launch the restore wizard. This will present you with the most recent restore point and an option to choose from others. If you choose this second option, the window that appears contains a "Show more restore points" check box in its bottom-left corner, as shown in Figure 5-3.

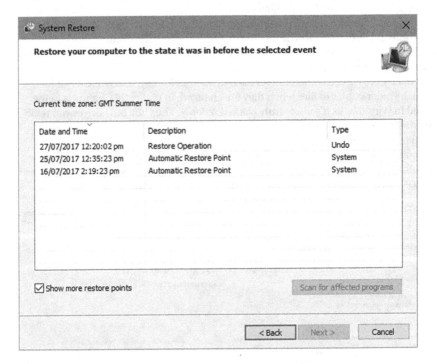

Figure 5-3. *You can view just the most recent or all available restore points*

If you need to further check what rolling back to a specific restore point will really do, highlight it and then click the "Scan for affected programs" button. This will display a complete list of all the software and drivers on your PC that would be affected, either rolled back to before and updated or removed completely, by the restore, as shown in Figure 5-4.

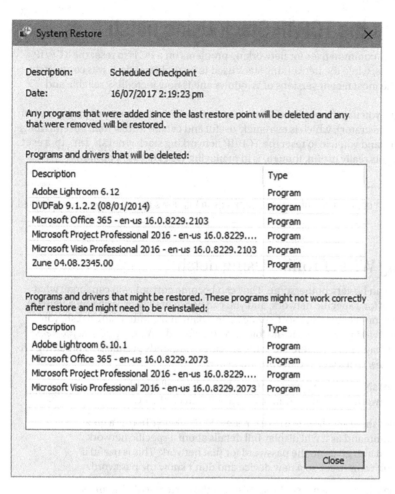

Figure 5-4. *You can see what will be affected by System Restore*

■ **Tip** You can run System Restore from the recovery tools if you have a nonbootable copy of Windows. Start the PC from your installation media, a System Repair Disc (Windows 7), or a Recovery Drive (Windows 8.1 and Windows 10), and select the Repair option. System Restore will be available as one of the options and works identically to how it does on the desktop.

Resetting the TCP/IP Stack Using netsh

One of the most common fixes for networking problems on a PC is to reset the TCP/IP stack. In fairness, while the networking stack used to be problematic, it was completely rewritten in the most recent versions of Windows and is now incredibly reliable and robust.

To do this, you use the netsh command from the Windows command prompt (when run as an administrator), which is extremely useful and can do a great many useful things.

The command you use to reset the TCP/IP networking stack is netsh int ip reset. Where netsh gets really useful, though, is in managing Wi-Fi network profiles.

■ **Tip**   You can get a full list of netsh commands in Windows at http://pcs.tv/2fo8Bed.

Managing Wi-Fi Profiles Using netsh

Wi-Fi profiles can be very bothersome. They can become corrupt, you can forget what the password is for a specific network, and you can accidentally misconfigure a network when you first connect to it. In short, they can be a pain in the butt. Using netsh, you can tame your Wi-Fi profiles using the following commands. We showed you the netsh command in Chapter 3, but there are some specific commands pertinent to repairing Wi-Fi network issues, so it's worth repeating them here.

- netsh wlan show profiles displays a list of all the Wi-Fi networks for which connections are stored on the PC.

- netsh wlan show profiles name="SSID" key=clear is a great command as it will display full details about a specific network and also give you the password for that network. This is useful if you want to set up a new device and don't know the password.

- netsh wlan show settings displays the current global settings for all of the PC's Wi-Fi network connections.

- netsh wlan show blockednetworks displays a list of any Wi-Fi profiles that have been specifically blocked using netsh.

- netsh wlan set blockednetworks display={show|hide} can be used to show or hide the display of blocked networks from the main networks list.

- netsh wlan add filter permission={allow|block|denyall} ssid="SSID" networktype={infrastructure|adhoc} allows or blocks a specific network.

- netsh wlan delete filter permission={allow|block|den yall} ssid="SSID" networktype={infrastructure|adhoc} deletes an allow, block, or denyall filter that's been applied to a network.

- `netsh wlan set profileorder name="SSID"`
  `interface="Network Interface Name" priority=1` sets the
  connection priority for a specific Wi-Fi network, so the ones you
  want used first will have the correct priority.

Windows Reset

Windows 10 includes a handy reimaging feature called Reset. It's an imaging tool that's really quite clever in how it works, though there are significant downsides too. (It's called Refresh in Windows 8.1, and it's absent from Windows 7 where you just have the System Image Backup tool.)

You run Reset (and Refresh) from the Update ➤ Security section of the Settings panel, where you'll find it in Recovery. What it does is reimage the PC from a backup, but the way it keeps this backup is clever because it is automatically updated to include all Windows Updates that are 30 days old or more. The theory, of course, is that if you've been using a PC with an update for 30 days, it can be considered stable and reliable.

The downside, however, is that you will have to reinstall and configure *all* of your installed software and apps. If you are using a PC running Windows 10 S or if you only use apps from the Windows Store or a Custom Business Store, then this isn't too much of a problem. If you have a lot of Win32 software installed, however, you might find the System Image Backup option more suitable for your needs.

Reset (Refresh) gives you two options when you run it: "Keep my files" and "Remove everything" and start again, as shown in Figure 5-5. The "Keep my files" option will make sure that any files and documents stored in the Users folder will be preserved.

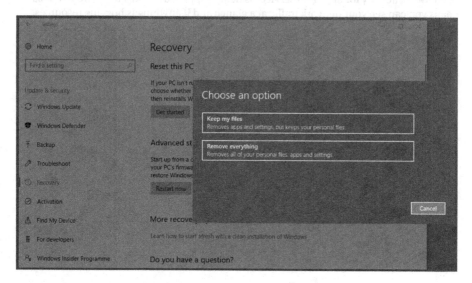

Figure 5-5. You can reset Windows 10 to recover from problems

89

> ■ **Note** We want to make a quick note about System Image Backup. This feature has now been deprecated by Microsoft in Windows 10. This means that while it will always remain in Windows 7 and Windows 8.1, it *may* be removed by Microsoft at some point in the future from Windows 10.

The Windows Administrative Tools

When it comes to reporting and diagnostics, the Windows administrative tools stand head and shoulders above anything else available in the OS. The level of detail you get from these tools is truly staggering. Here we'll show you how to use the tools and utilities most pertinent to networking troubleshooting.

Task Manager

We're going to begin with something that's not strictly an administrative tool but that is still relevant in many ways, the Task Manager. You're probably familiar with this already, but it's launched by right-clicking the taskbar or by performing a Ctrl+Alt+Del operation. In Windows 7 it's a fairly basic affair, but in Windows 8.1 and Windows 10 it has a few extra tricks up its sleeve.

On the Processes tab in the Task Manager, you will see that all CPU, memory, disk, and network activity for apps and services is heat-mapped, as shown in Figure 5-6. This means you can see your network traffic at a glance and if anything is hogging resources.

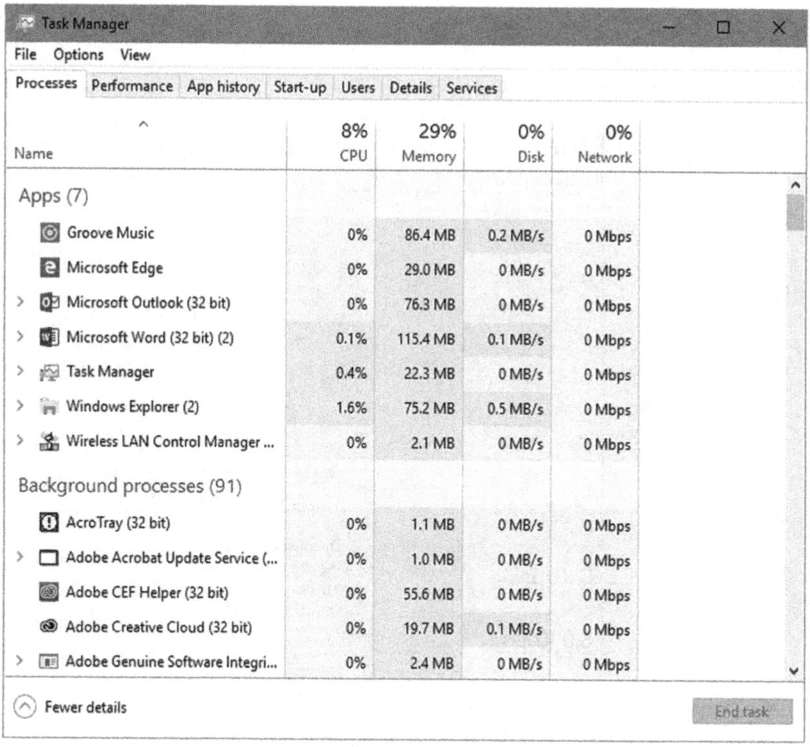

Name	8% CPU	29% Memory	0% Disk	0% Network	
Apps (7)					
Groove Music	0%	86.4 MB	0.2 MB/s	0 Mbps	
Microsoft Edge	0%	29.0 MB	0 MB/s	0 Mbps	
> Microsoft Outlook (32 bit)	0%	76.3 MB	0 MB/s	0 Mbps	
> Microsoft Word (32 bit) (2)	0.1%	115.4 MB	0.1 MB/s	0 Mbps	
> Task Manager	0.4%	22.3 MB	0 MB/s	0 Mbps	
> Windows Explorer (2)	1.6%	75.2 MB	0.5 MB/s	0 Mbps	
> Wireless LAN Control Manager ...	0%	2.1 MB	0 MB/s	0 Mbps	
Background processes (91)					
AcroTray (32 bit)	0%	1.1 MB	0 MB/s	0 Mbps	
> Adobe Acrobat Update Service (...	0%	1.0 MB	0 MB/s	0 Mbps	
Adobe CEF Helper (32 bit)	0%	55.6 MB	0 MB/s	0 Mbps	
Adobe Creative Cloud (32 bit)	0%	19.7 MB	0.1 MB/s	0 Mbps	
> Adobe Genuine Software Integri...	0%	2.4 MB	0 MB/s	0 Mbps	

Figure 5-6. Apps and services are heat-mapped by activity in the Task Manager

The Performance tab will display your current network activity as a live graph, with details of how much actual data is being sent and received by the PC at that time, as shown in Figure 5-7.

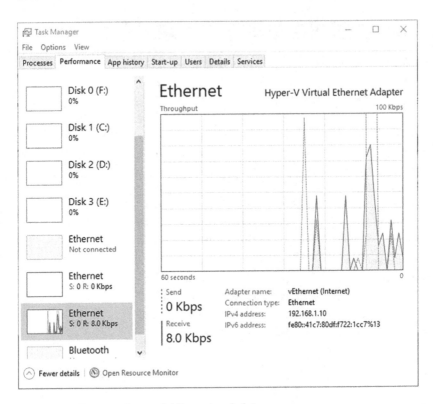

Figure 5-7. *You can view useful live network data*

Lastly, and this comes back to heat-mapping, the App history tab will show you how much total CPU, network, and metered network (aka cellular data) apps have been using over a period of time, as shown in Figure 5-8. You can use this to see what apps are consuming network resources on the PC.

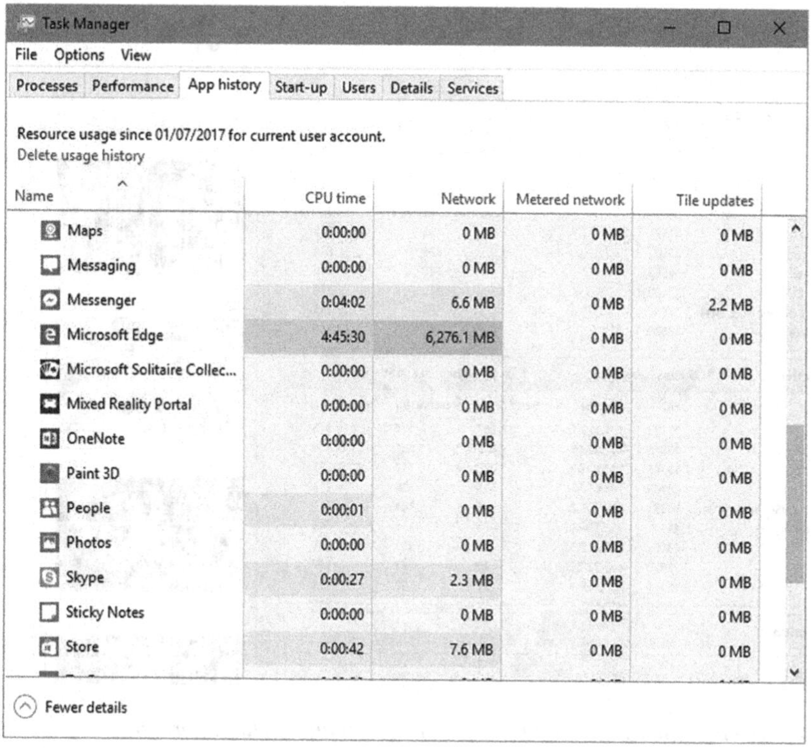
Task Manager
File Options View
Processes Performance App history Start-up Users Details Services
Resource usage since 01/07/2017 for current user account.
Delete usage history
Name
CPU time
Network
Metered network
Tile updates
Maps 0:00:00 0 MB 0 MB 0 MB
Messaging 0:00:00 0 MB 0 MB 0 MB
Messenger 0:04:02 6.6 MB 0 MB 2.2 MB
Microsoft Edge 4:45:30 6,276.1 MB 0 MB 0 MB
Microsoft Solitaire Collec... 0:00:00 0 MB 0 MB 0 MB
Mixed Reality Portal 0:00:00 0 MB 0 MB 0 MB
OneNote 0:00:00 0 MB 0 MB 0 MB
Paint 3D 0:00:00 0 MB 0 MB 0 MB
People 0:00:01 0 MB 0 MB 0 MB
Photos 0:00:00 0 MB 0 MB 0 MB
Skype 0:00:27 2.3 MB 0 MB 0 MB
Sticky Notes 0:00:00 0 MB 0 MB 0 MB
Store 0:00:42 7.6 MB 0 MB 0 MB
Fewer details

Figure 5-8. *You can track greedy apps in the Task Manager*

Resource Monitor

The first administrative tool to detail here is one that's linked directly from the bottom of the Performance tab in the Task Manager. The Resource Monitor takes the reporting of the Task Manager and scales it up.

The Performance Monitor consists of five tabs, each containing collapsible panels. The Overview tab contains panels displaying the apps, drivers, and services currently using the PC's CPU, disk, networking, and memory, though switching to one of the other tabs across the top of the window presents much more useful information.

For example, in Figure 5-9 you can see the Network tab open. Here there are collapsible panels including Processes with Network Activity, Network Activity, TCP Connections, and Listening Ports.

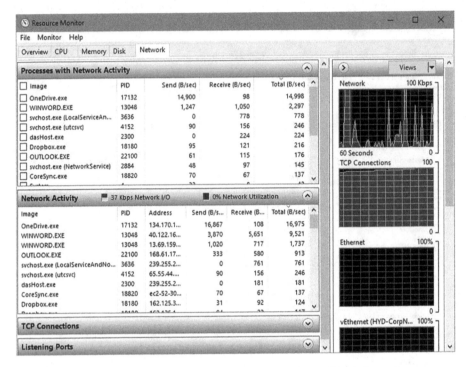

Figure 5-9. *The Performance Monitor provides huge amounts of live information*

Each of the processes using the network on your PC has a check box to the left of its name. By checking an app or service, the rest of the panels will change to show only network information relevant to that particular process, so you can check what it's doing, knowing that you won't miss anything.

Additionally, the Network Activity and TCP Connections panels will detail the IP address, network name, or domain name of the resource being accessed so you can see what processes are communicating with the outside world or across your network.

Performance Monitor

The Performance Monitor is similar to the Resource Monitor in some ways, in that it provides live data about what's happening on your PC. However, the Performance Monitor allows you to display the data according to OS function instead of process activity.

For example, if you click the green plus (+) icon to add a counter, or counters, to the graph and navigate to Network Interface, you will see a whole long list of network functions that you can display for all network adapters in the PC or that you can narrow to a single adapter, as shown in Figure 5-10.

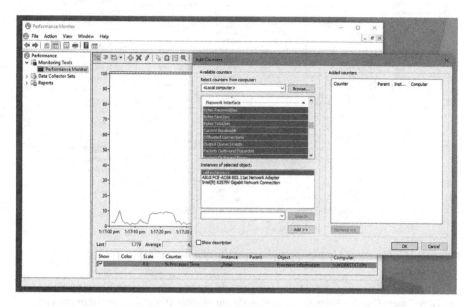

Figure 5-10. *The Performance Monitor provides live information about your PC*

If you need to keep an eye on specific OS functions, then the Performance Monitor is an excellent tool for doing so.

Event Viewer

Almost nothing happens on a PC without it being recorded in the Windows Event Viewer. This reporting utility separates events into Information, Warnings, Errors, and Critical [Errors]. Each event is clickable and comes with a text description of what happened, along with the time and date of the event and any error codes (in the format 0x000000) that you can search for online, as shown in Figure 5-11.

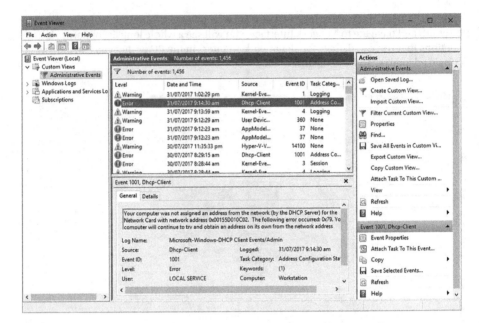

Figure 5-11. *The Event Monitor provides a wealth of information*

There are some very useful things you can do in the Event Viewer, however. You can click Create Custom View in the right-side panel. This allows you to gather data on a specific operating system function so you can track errors and events over time, as shown in Figure 5-12.

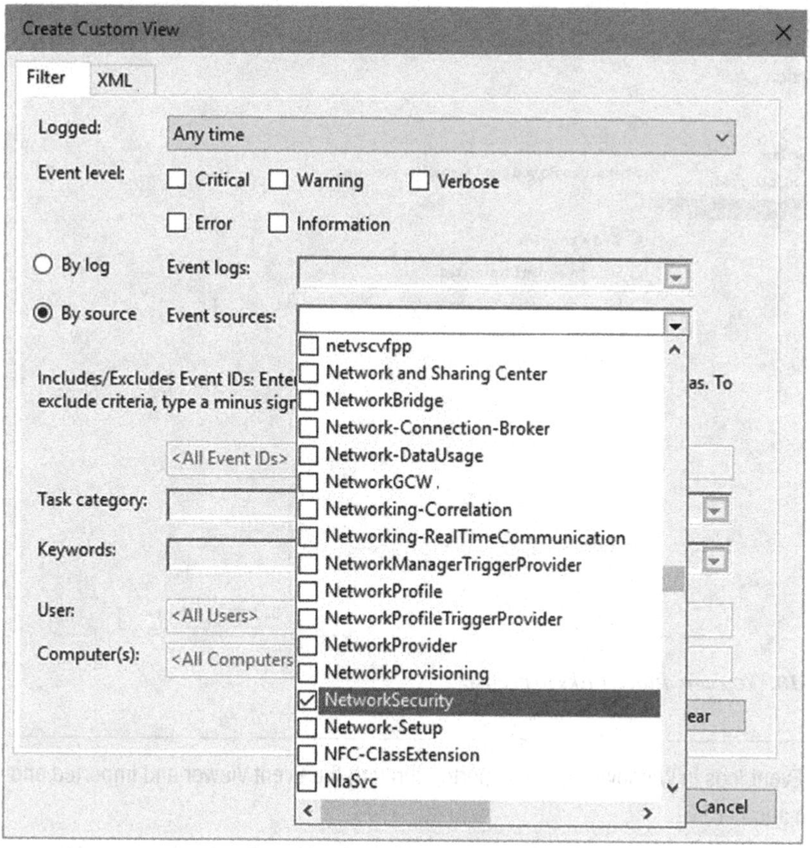

Figure 5-12. *You can create custom views to gather data*

Also in the right panel is a Filter Current [Custom] View option that you can use to filter any custom view you have created so that you can narrow down the data contained within it.

Once you have determined what event or error you want to track, you can select Attach Task To This Event by highlighting it and then clicking the correct option near the bottom-right corner of the window.

The reason to attach a task to an event is that you might want to start a program such as an automated troubleshooter, as shown in Figure 5-13; send an e-mail to a support person (you don't need an e-mail client on the PC, just a valid SMTP address that the Event Viewer can use to send the mail); or display a message on the PC's screen, such as one telling the user to stop what they're doing and call support so they can describe exactly what's running at that time.

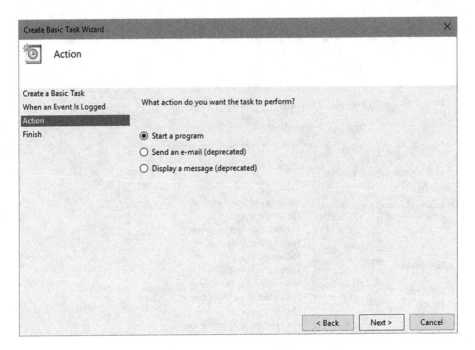

Figure 5-13. *You can attach tasks to events*

▮ **Tip**   Event logs in Windows can be exported through the Event Viewer and imported and viewed on another PC.

System Information

Sometimes you need detailed information about the PC, and you can get this in the System Information panel. This will provide extremely detailed, exportable information about the PC and everything installed on it, as shown in Figure 5-14.

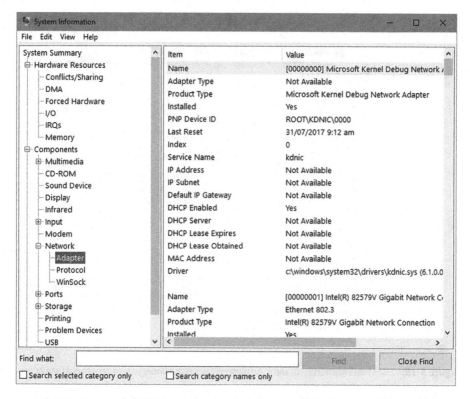

Figure 5-14. *You can get detailed information about the PC from System Information*

Firewall with Advanced Security

The last administrative tool we'll discuss is the Windows Firewall with Advanced Security. Sometimes you might find that network activity is being blocked by the firewall, perhaps because you have custom software, a secure connection that requires a specific port to be open, or a specific service that requires network access that's currently denied.

The Windows Firewall with Advanced Security allows you to specify individual rules for inbound and outbound network traffic on the PC, categorized by Program, Port, or Predefined (basically a master list of Windows features), or to create a fully custom rule, as shown in Figure 5-15.

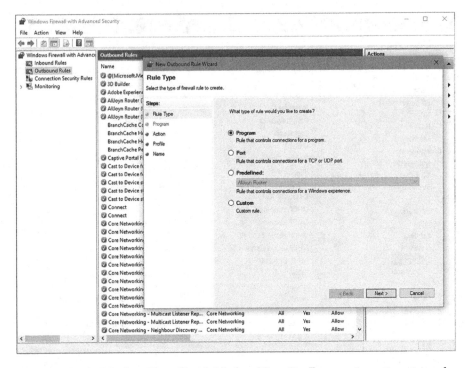

Figure 5-15. *The Windows Firewall with Advanced Security allows you to create custom rules*

Additionally, you can create connection security rules that will allow you to specify the security, authentication, and peer-to-peer technologies and addresses for secure business networks.

Microsoft SysInternals Suite

Microsoft provides a suite of advanced diagnostic and reporting tools for Windows in its SysInternals Suite, which is available from http://technet.microsoft.com/ sysinternals. This suite includes specific network reporting tools, plus some extra utilities that are utterly invaluable to any IT professional. These are the main networking tools for troubleshooting:

- PsPing is more configurable than the standard Windows ping command. You can use this to test network connections.

- PsTools is a suite of tools for remotely administering other PCs on a network.

- TCPView provides detailed information about endpoint network connections, including IP addresses and port data, as shown in Figure 5-16.

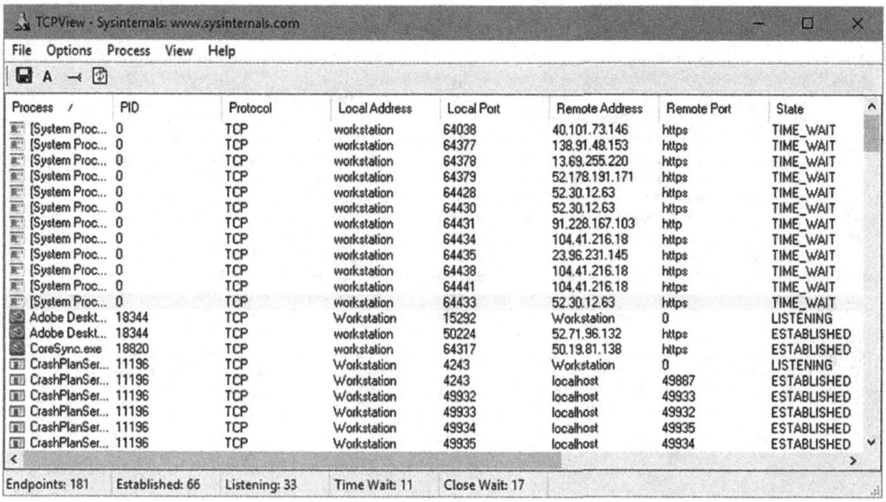

Figure 5-16. *TCPView provides detailed information about network connections*

- WhoIs is a handy utility for reporting on the registered owner of domain names or IP addresses online.

There are a few SysInternals utilities, though, that we want to highlight for their out-and-out usefulness.

Autoruns

Earlier in this chapter we detailed the Resource Monitor, which you can use to see everything running on the PC. Where it can't help, though, is when you have a rogue process, such as a DLL or service that's running at startup and hogging or causing other problems with network traffic.

That's where Autoruns comes in, as shown in Figure 5-17. This brilliant utility details absolutely everything that runs when the PC starts, including Registry keys, DLLs, and more besides. You can use this to disable anything that might be causing problems on the PC.

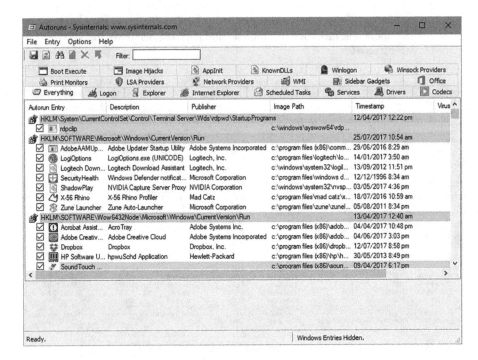

Figure 5-17. *Autoruns details everything that runs at startup*

Process Explorer

The next two aren't specifically network tools, but they're so useful you never know when you might need them. Process Explorer, as shown in Figure 5-18, will detail what program has opened a particular file or directory, as well as detailing process dependencies and associated Registry keys for a process.

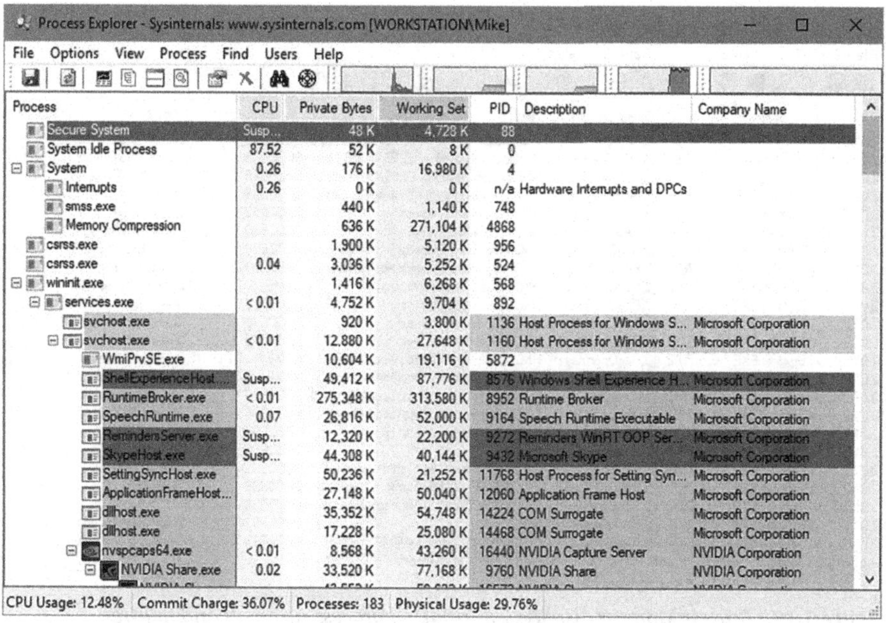

Figure 5-18. *Process Explorer displays details on running processes on the PC*

Process Monitor

Process Monitor, on the other hand, shows real-time information for file system, Registry, and process activity, as shown in Figure 5-19. This makes it easy to get detailed information on individual activities that are impacting the PC at that time.

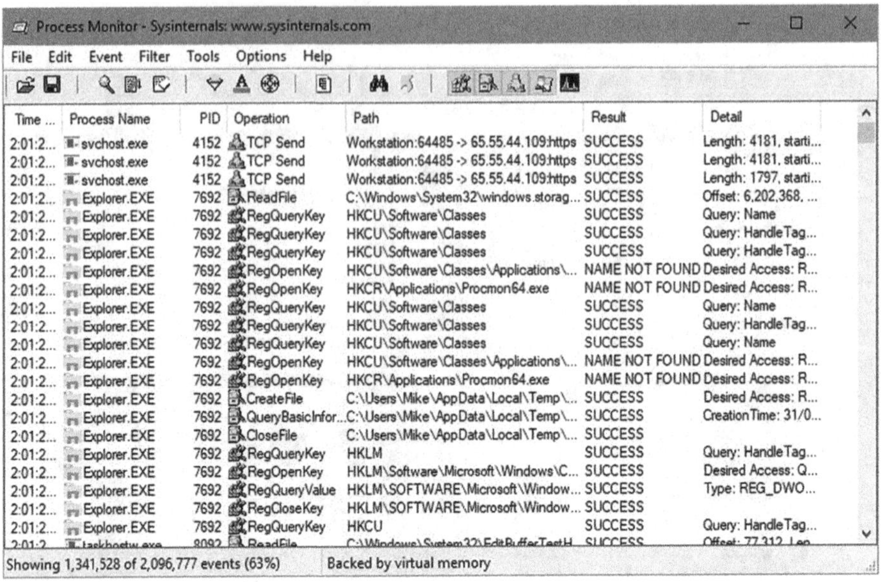

Figure 5-19. Process Monitor displays information process successes and failures

Microsoft Network Monitor

Outside of the SysInternals Suite there are also additional useful tools that are provided by Microsoft. Microsoft Network Monitor is an archived product but still available from the Microsoft web site at http://pcs.tv/2tW2Hui. It is used to view the contents of data packets that are being sent and received over the network.

Microsoft Message Analyzer

The Microsoft Message Analyzer has replaced the Microsoft Network Monitor. You can download it from http://pcs.tv/2uQnywt, and you can use it to analyze data packets sent across the network as well as to view much more detailed information than the Network Monitor can provide on exactly is being sent and received across your network.

Managing Roaming Network Profiles

Sometimes a PC connected to a company domain can experience corruption in what's called the *roaming profile*. This is the user's specific connection settings to the server and their configuration and customization options. If this happens, you can delete the roaming profile and re-create it the next time the user connects to the domain server.

To do this, open System from the Control Panel and then click Advanced System Settings. On the Advanced tab, you will see a User Profiles section, as shown in Figure 5-20. Click the Settings button, and a dialog will appear containing both local and roaming user profiles that are stored on the PC. You can use this dialog box to change profiles between local and roaming and also to delete a corrupt profile.

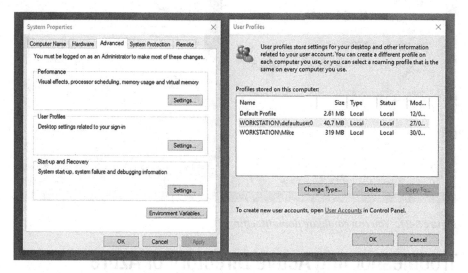

Figure 5-20. *You can delete corrupt roaming domain profiles*

Managing Domain Settings

Additionally, you can manage the domain settings themselves from the System properties panel by clicking the Computer Name tab and then the Change button. Here a dialog will appear where you can specify whether the computer is attached to a workgroup or a domain, as shown in Figure 5-21. You can use this if the domain settings are incorrect or misconfigured.

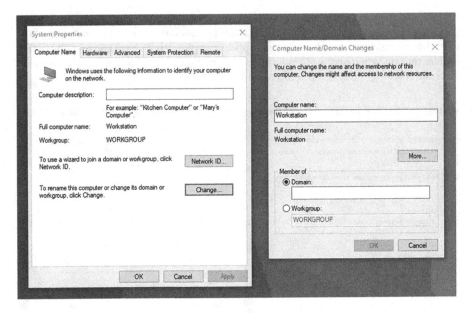

Figure 5-21. *You can configure domain settings*

Troubleshooting Active Directory or Azure

If you are using Windows 10, there is a useful feature to help you troubleshoot problems with Active Directory or Microsoft Azure connections. In the Settings panel, navigate to Accounts and then "Access work or school." Here a link called "Export your management log files" will save Event log files to your users' folder. These log files can be viewed to check for any connection problems and errors that may be occurring.

Summary

There's a lot that can be done in Windows to troubleshoot and repair network problems, and the reporting and configuration tools that are available can provide so much information that it's incredibly helpful that they can all be filtered to display only the specific information you require in the real world.

In the next chapter, though, you're going to take a step from the real into the virtual. This doesn't mean you'll need a VR headset to read it; you'll look in depth at how you configure, manage, and troubleshoot networks in Hyper-V and Azure.

CHAPTER 6

■ ■ ■

Networking in a Virtual World

Years ago, setting up and running a network in a large enterprise meant purchasing lots of computers. Each computer had a single job to do. Client computers ran an operating system and either were assigned to single users or were configured for multiple users through additional user accounts. Servers ran a single operating system and were configured to manage something specific. Some were created for Active Directory management only, some managed data, and others managed resources.

Nowadays, though, that's not the way it's done. Enterprises purchase fewer machines, and the machines they do purchase are powerful. They virtualize on those machines to use their resources more wisely. There's virtualization in the cloud too; not all resources need be on-site.

In this chapter, we'll focus on virtualization technologies. We'll discuss Hyper-V for the most part. Hyper-V is a role in Windows Server that lets you create the virtualized environments on your own computers. We'll also offer a brief introduction to Windows Azure, which offers cloud computing platform and services, and can also be used to create virtual machines.

Understanding Hyper-V

Microsoft's solution to virtualization is Hyper-V. You use Hyper-V to create and manage virtual machines. A virtual machine acts and feels like a single, physical, stand-alone computer but is generally hosted by a computer that also supports other virtual systems. By virtualizing resources in this manner, companies save time, money, and even space when creating and managing networks. Imagine being able to take, say, a dozen physical machines and virtualize them into one. Not only are you limiting the hardware you use, but you're making it easier to manage those systems by making them available from a single location. Each of the virtual machines can have one or multiple roles as well, so the need for specialty servers is reduced.

With Hyper-V you can also establish a virtual desktop infrastructure when you add the Remote Desktop Virtualization Host on the same server. This enables you to create virtual desktop pools for workers. You can then have users log in to these virtual workstations, again freeing up resources and reducing the need for additional hardware. Additionally, you manage those desktops from a single location, making them easier to reinstall and update when needed.

© Mike Halsey and Joli Ballew 2017
M. Halsey and J. Ballew, *Windows Networking Troubleshooting*,
https://doi.org/10.1007/978-1-4842-3222-4_6

Of course, there are other reasons to use virtualization. You can create a virtual system for testing and research and development. Virtual systems are isolated from other systems, so there's no chance you'll disrupt the network. You can incorporate cloud virtualization with on-site virtualization as well and grow your business effectively. You can easily reinstall operating systems or revert to a previous, stable time through the use of checkpoints too.

Features of Hyper-V

There are some features of Hyper-V that we don't want to go unnoticed. One is that each virtual machine includes options you can configure for memory, processor, storage, and networking. A virtual server, for instance, could be configured to have access to a lot of memory and hard drive space, while a virtual desktop could be configured to use much less. It's like building your own physical machine—you pick the specs!

Hyper-V offers optimization features too. Each guest operating system can be migrated even when live and so can its storage areas. This means you don't have to take the machine offline to move it. There are commands inside the virtual machine interface for both importing and exporting to make this easy. Each virtual machine has a set of integration services too, which includes various services and drivers to assist in integration processes between the virtual machine (VM) and the host. Additionally, Hyper-V Replica creates copies of your machine for backup.

If desired, administrators can access the Hyper-V machines remotely. This isn't just Remote Desktop, which you might be used to; this type of connection offers a console you can use to be more effective and allows you to access the machine even if it isn't booted.

■ **Note**   Virtual machines are a great option for running legacy operating systems in a safe space.

Hyper-V Requirements and Compatible OSs

You can install Hyper-V on both Server OSs and some 64-bit Windows clients. Here's a summary of the host machines that support Hyper-V and can thus serve as hosts for multiple virtual machines:

- Hyper-V is available on 64-bit versions of Windows Professional, Enterprise, and Education in Windows 8 and later.

- Hyper-V is not available on any Windows Home edition.

- Hyper-V is available on Windows Server 2008; Windows Server 2008 R2 Standard, Enterprise, and Datacenter editions; and Windows Server 2012 Standard and Datacenter editions.

- Hyper-V is available in Server 2016 Standard and Datacenter editions.

- Hyper-V is not available on any pre-Server 2012 OSs.

- Hyper-V is available on Microsoft Hyper-V Server 2016, which is a stand-alone product that contains only the Windows hypervisor and other necessary virtualization components. It can also support virtual machines and serve as a host computer.

■ **Note**   At the time this book was written, you could opt to move your on-site Windows Server licenses with Software Assurance to Windows Azure to enable a hybrid cloud model at a reduced rate. If you're thinking of using Azure, consider checking for specials like these before making any new investments in server licenses.

Additionally, the computers that run Hyper-V and serve as virtual machine hosts must meet the following requirements and have the following components:

- A 64-bit processor with second-level address translation (SLAT).

- VM Monitor Mode extensions.

- At least 4GB of RAM. More is better. Remember, you'll be sharing this memory among your virtual machines.

- Virtualization support enabled in the BIOS or UEFI.

- Hardware-assisted virtualization and hardware-enforced Data Execution Prevention (DEP) must be enabled.

Regarding the guest OSs, you can install just about any guest operating system on the virtual machines you create. In Server 2016, supported guest operating systems include OSs from Windows 7 and Windows Server 2008 with Service Pack 2 forward. Additionally, Hyper-V supports Linux and FreeBSD virtual machines.

To see whether a specific computer can support Hyper-V, follow these steps:

1. Open Windows PowerShell or a command prompt.

2. Type **Systeminfo.exe** and press Enter.

3. In the resulting report, scroll to the Hyper-V Requirements section.

4. Verify that a hypervisor has been detected, as shown in Figure 6-1.

```
                      [03]: KB4034074
Network Card(s):      3 NIC(s) Installed.
                      [01]: Realtek PCIe GBE Family Controller
                            Connection Name: Ethernet 2
                            Status:          Media disconnected
                      [02]: Intel(R) Dual Band Wireless-AC 7265
                            Connection Name: Wi-Fi
                            DHCP Enabled:    Yes
                            DHCP Server:     192.168.1.1
                            IP address(es)
                            [01]: 192.168.1.250
                            [02]: fe80::35a9:3a5:789:e406
                      [03]: Bluetooth Device (Personal Area Network)
                            Connection Name: Bluetooth Network Connection
                            Status:          Media disconnected
Hyper-V Requirements: A hypervisor has been detected. Features required for I
PS C:\Users\joli_>
```

Figure 6-1. This shows that a hypervisor has been detected

Installing Hyper-V

You need to install Hyper-V before you can use it. So, once you know you are running a compatible operating system and that a hypervisor is available, you're just about ready to go. Take a minute first to make sure you enable virtualization support in the BIOS or UEFI if it isn't enabled already and that the other virtualization requirements outlined earlier have been met as well.

Installing on Server 2016

There are several steps to installing Hyper-V on Server 2016, and installing on other server editions is similar. You install Hyper-V through Server Manager by following these steps:

1. Open Server Manager.

2. Click Manage and then Add Roles and Features, as shown in Figure 6-2.

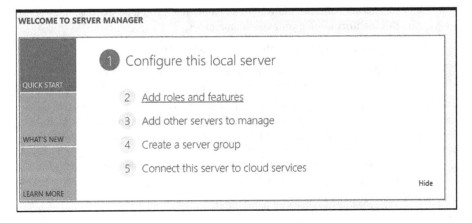

Figure 6-2. Adding roles and features in Server Manager

3. Verify the computer meets the requirements and is configured correctly and then click Next.

4. Select "Role-based or feature-based installation." Click Next.

5. Select a server and then click Next.

6. Select Hyper-V.

7. Click Add Features and click Next.

8. On the next three pages (Create Virtual Switches, Virtual Machine Migration, and Default Stores), select the appropriate options.

9. Select "Restart the destination server automatically if required."

10. Click Install.

Installing on Windows 10

There are several ways to install Hyper-V on Windows 10. One is to use the following command in an elevated PowerShell window: Enable-WindowsOptionalFeature -Online -FeatureName:Microsoft-Hyper-V -All. Another is to use a graphical interface. We prefer the interface option because it's easy to tell just what kind of Hyper-V support the computer has.

To enable Hyper-V on a Windows 10 machine, follow these steps:

1. Navigate to Control Panel ➤ Programs ➤ Programs and Features.

2. Select Turn Windows Features on or off.

3. Click the + sign next to Hyper-V.

4. If you can select the first option, Hyper-V is supported. If you can select all three, the computer can host its own Hyper-V machines. See Figure 6-3.

Figure 6-3. Install Hyper-V support and/or the Hyper-V Management Tools and Platform

5. Click OK.

6. Restart the computer.

Creating a Virtual Machine

With the Hyper-V Platform and Hyper-V Management Tools installed, you can now create your first virtual machine. We prefer the graphical user interface over any other options, such as PowerShell, so that's what we'll outline here.

Let's start with Windows 10. (Creating a virtual machine on any Windows Server is almost the same.)

On Windows 10

To create a virtual machine on Windows 10, you work through a wizard. During this process, you will be prompted to make choices about the machine you want to configure. Some of the decisions you'll make depend on the type of operating system you want to install, what kind of hardware you have access to, the amount of resources available (RAM, HD, etc.), and similar confines. Although we could spell out each option in paragraph form here, we believe the best way to learn about these options is to go through the wizard.

To create a virtual machine on a Windows 10 computer, explore the default settings and install an OS.

1. Open Hyper-V Manager. You can search for it from the Search window on the taskbar.

2. Click Action ➤ New ➤ Virtual Machine. See Figure 6-4.

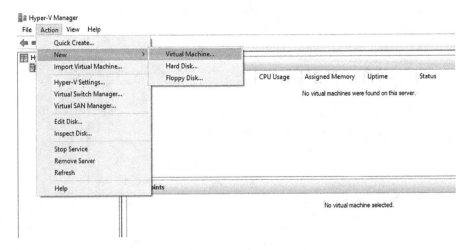

Figure 6-4. *Create a new virtual machine from the Action menu*

3. Click Next to begin.

4. Type a name for your virtual machine. This could be the name of the operating system you'll install on it. Click Next.

5. Read what's offered and choose Generation 1 or Generation 2, as shown in Figure 6-5. Generation 1 is always a safe bet. Generation 2 requires newer virtualization features and a 64-bit guest OS. Click Next.

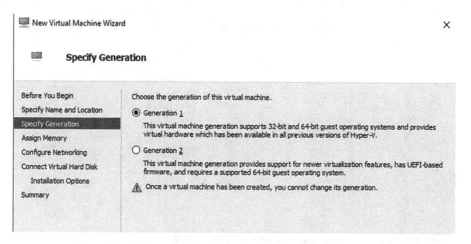

Figure 6-5. Choose the generation type for the virtual machine

6. Type how much memory to allot. The default is 1024MB. We suggest at least doubling that.

7. Accept the Connection option of Not Connected unless you already have a network adapter configured for use with a virtual machine. If you do, select it. You'll learn to create an adapter later in this chapter if you don't see one here. Click Next.

8. Review and then accept the defaults for connecting a virtual hard disk (unless you have a specific reason not to) and click Next.

9. Click Install an Operating System from a Bootable CD/DVD and do one of the following:

    a. Choose Physical CD/DVD Drive and select the drive to use.

    b. Choose Image File (.iso) and click Browse to locate the file to open. Click Open when you find it.

10. Review the settings and click Finish.

11. In the Hyper-V Manager window, verify the new virtual machine exists. Right-click to access the options. See Figure 6-6.

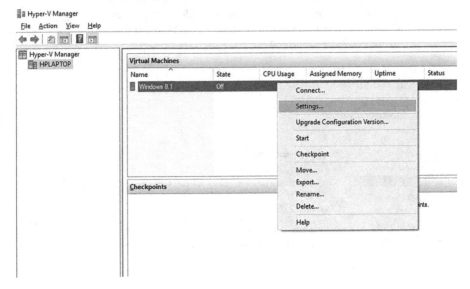

Figure 6-6. *Hyper-V Manager shows the new virtual machine*

To complete the installation of the operating system, follow these steps:

1. As shown in Figure 6-6, right-click the virtual machine to access the options.

2. Click Connect.

3. Click Start.

4. The operating system installation file will load. Complete the installation as prompted. See Figure 6-7.

▪ **Note** Performing an OS installation on a virtual machine is exactly like performing one on a physical machine.

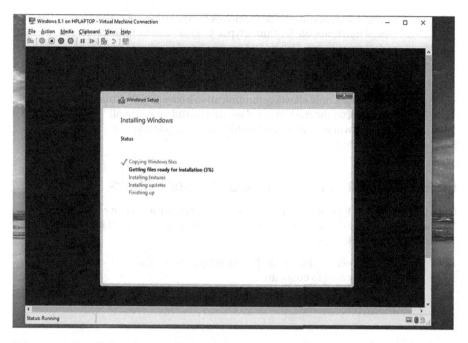

Figure 6-7. Install the operating system on the virtual machine

On Server 2012 and Server 2016

Creating virtual machines hasn't changed much over the years. Creating them on Server 2016 is almost exactly like creating them on Server 2012 and Windows 10. When you're ready, return to the steps for Windows 10 shown earlier and open Hyper-V Manager on your server. Work through the wizard as prompted, configuring the generation type, memory settings, and so on, and installing an operating system.

Creating a Virtual Switch

A virtual switch is what allows your new virtual machine to connect to other virtual machines, your local network, or the Internet. Thus, creating a virtual switch is the next step in the creation process. Before you create a switch, you need to decide what type you want. There are three types of switches.

- *External*: This allows virtual machines to access a physical network. Use this switch to connect to servers, clients, and the Internet through the host's network adapter. This also allows the virtual machine to communicate with the other virtual machines hosted on the same Hyper-V server.

- *Internal*: This allows virtual machines to communicate with other virtual machines on the same Hyper-V server and communicate with the server too. Use this when the virtual machine doesn't need access to the Internet or external network but still needs access to the host computer.

- *Private*: This only allows communication between the virtual machines on the host Hyper-V server. It is isolated from all other networks and network traffic. Use this option in test environments.

Create a Switch in Windows 10 and Other Editions

Once you know what type of switch you want, you can create it in Hyper-V Manager. The steps are virtually the same from Server 2012 and up and Windows 8.1 and up. To create a switch, follow these steps:

1. Open Hyper-V Manager and in the left pane click the computer host to configure.

2. Click Action ➤ Virtual Switch Manager, as shown in Figure 6-8.

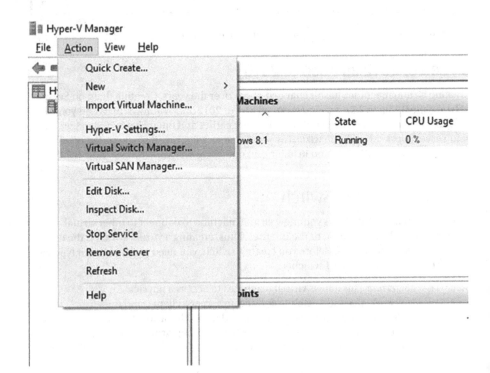

Figure 6-8. Use the Virtual Switch Manager to create a switch

3. Choose the type of switch you want.

4. Click Create Virtual Switch.

5. Type a name for the switch.

6. If you have chosen to create an external switch, you'll have to select a network adapter to use. It's likely already selected. Read the other information offered and make changes if desired; usually the defaults are fine.

7. Click OK.

8. Click Yes if prompted that you might lose network connectivity.

9. If the switch can't be created, return to step 6 and select another network adapter, if one is available.

To view your new switch, follow these steps:

1. Right-click the Network icon on the taskbar.

2. Click Open Network and Sharing Center.

3. Click Change Adapter Settings.

4. Note the new switch in the Network Connections window. See Figure 6-9.

Figure 6-9. *The new switch appears in the Network Connections window*

Exploring Hyper-V Management Tools

Once you've set up Hyper-V and configured a virtual machine, you have several management options. If you want to use a graphical interface, you should opt for Hyper-V Manager. The most common settings are available from Hyper-V Settings, and it's fairly easy to perform tasks on the machines you create.

There are also tools for connecting to and managing virtual machines, specifically the Virtual Machine Connection options. With these, you can start and shut down the machine, connect to a DVD image or USB drive for installation, create checkpoints, and modify settings, among other things.

Additional options for managing your virtual machines include Hyper-V for Windows PowerShell and Windows PowerShell Direct. These tools involve learning commands and syntax, but as you might suspect, they also provide a way to perform tasks that aren't available using any other method.

Hyper-V Settings

You've been introduced to Hyper-V Manager. It's where you created your first virtual machine and where you created its virtual switch. There are other settings you haven't explored yet, though. Those are available from the Hyper-V Settings option either from the Action menu or from the right pane of Hyper-V Manager. Figure 6-10 shows the option in the right pane and the resulting window that appears after clicking there.

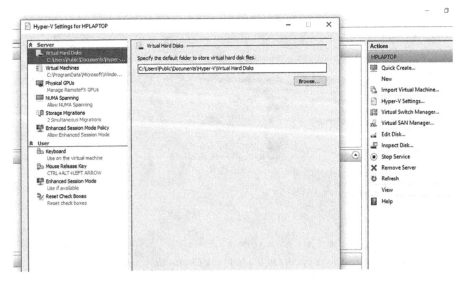

Figure 6-10. Hyper-V Settings are available from the right pane of Hyper-V Manager

In Figure 6-10, notice that Virtual Hard Disks is selected in the left pane. To the right of that you'll see the default folder for storing virtual hard disk files. Yes, they are files! This means you can choose where you'd like to save them if you don't like the default location. Simply click Browse.

As you work your way down the list, you'll see some other things you can do. The second entry enables you to specify the default folder for the virtual machine's configuration files. The third entry, Physical GPUs, lets you choose which graphics processing units (GPUs) you want to use. Many computers come with more than one. Here are the highlights of the remaining entries under Server:

- *NUMA Spanning*: Non-Uniform Memory Architecture (NUMA) is a technology you can enable that allows virtual machines to span available NUMA nodes to provide additional computing resources. This helps you run more than one virtual machine at a time and can provide them with more memory than what is available on a single node.

- *Storage Migrations*: A storage migration lets you move, service, and upgrade storage resources even if the virtual machine affected is running. Here you specify how many simultaneous migrations are allowed.

- *Enhanced Session Mode*: This offers support for the redirection of local resources to a virtual machine session. It's like the redirection you might be used to from a Remote Desktop (RDP) session. This enables the virtual machine to access the required or desired resources such as printers, the clipboard, or USB drives. If you enable this, you can configure settings for the resources you want to access as outlined next.

- Under User, there are additional settings and options. Click Keyboard to configure the following options for the VM:

  - *Keyboard*: The settings here apply to key combinations such as Alt+C and Ctrl+Alt+Del. You can opt to apply the key combinations you use to the local computer (host), to the virtual machine, or to the virtual machine only when it's in full-screen mode.

  - *Mouse Release Key*: Specify the key combination you want to use to release the mouse when the virtual machine drivers are not installed. You use this with the virtual machine connection. Figure 6-11 shows the options.

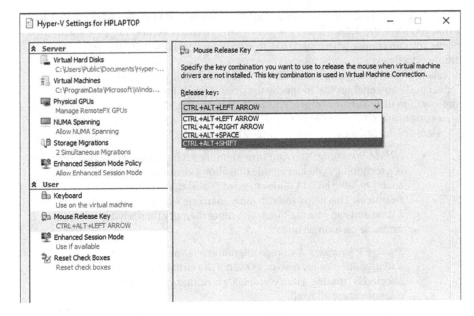

Figure 6-11. *Mouse Release Key settings in Hyper-V Settings*

- *Enhanced Session Mode*: As noted earlier, this enables enhanced session mode for the virtual machine.

- *Reset Check Boxes*: Click Reset here to return all check boxes, warning boxes, confirmation messages, and so on, to their original states.

Virtual Machine Settings

If you've installed an operating system on your virtual machine, there are settings available to you for working with that OS. These include the option to add hardware, create checkpoints, reconfigure memory settings, and so much more. There are various ways to access these options, but one way is, again, from inside Hyper-V Manager and from the right pane.

Before we start, look back at Figure 6-10. Under HP Laptop in the right pane you see the option Hyper-V Settings. We just explored those settings. Notice that there is nothing listed under the HPLaptop Help option. Now look at Figure 6-12. While writing these last few pages, we've installed an operating system on the virtual disk we created earlier. Now you can see that there are more entries in that right pane. Specifically, they are entries related to the operating system installed on the disk, Windows 8.1.

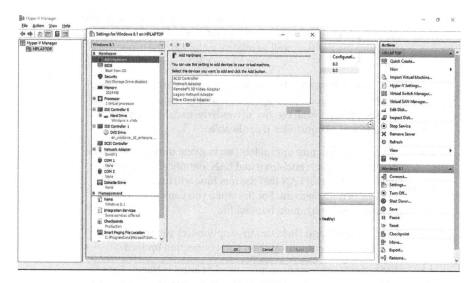

Figure 6-12. *Settings for the OS are available from the right pane (under the name of the virtual machine) and the resulting Settings window*

To access the settings for Windows 8.1 (or whatever OS you installed), click Settings. You'll see the window shown in Figure 6-12. As you can see, there are lots of options. Let's look at each of these briefly.

Under the Hardware section you'll find the Add Hardware option listed first. This lets you install hardware onto your virtual machine. Click anything you'd like to add. Yes, it looks like it's grayed out, but you can still click there. You could, for instance, install a network adapter if you were unable to create a switch earlier.

Here are the additional options with short descriptions of their purpose:

- The BIOS option lets you select the order in which the virtual machine should look for boot devices. This is just what a "real" computer does, and the settings are the same. As far as the host machine or virtual machine knows, it is a real, physical computer. If you can't access these settings, in the virtual machine select File ➤ Exit and then close and reopen the Settings window. This holds true for some of the other settings too.

- The Security option lets you secure the virtual machine with encryption, provided you've also installed a key storage drive. There's an option here to learn more about key encryption security, if that's something you'd like to set up.

- The Memory option lets you set the minimum and maximum RAM that the virtual machine can use. You can also set a memory buffer limit and specify a priority setting for this virtual machine.

- The Processor option lets you configure what processors are used and how, if more than one processor exists on the host. You can configure the limits as well as relative weight for the processors you select.

- IDE Controller options let you add hard drives and DVD drives, inspect media, point to image files, and select specific drives for installations and even remove drives if desired. You can also add drives to a SCSI controller, if applicable.

- The Network Adapter option lets you manage the virtual switches you create. You can enable virtual LAN identification, which specifies the virtual LAN that the machine will use, and enable bandwidth management. For the latter, you can configure minimum and maximum bandwidth.

- COM 1, COM2, and Diskette Drive options let you specify and configure these communication and connection options.

- Under the Management section, the first entry is Name. There's not much to see here, just the option to change the name of the virtual machine and write some notes about it.

- The Integration Services option lets you select services that you want Hyper-V to offer the virtual machine. The Guest OS must support these options, and they include the following:

  - *Operating System Shutdown*: This allows the Hyper-V administrator to shut down the virtual machines without having to log into it.

  - *Time Synchronization*: This lets the machine synchronize its time with its host.

  - *Data Exchange*: This allows for the sharing of information (data) between the host and the virtual machine.

  - *Heartbeat*: This allows the Heartbeat service to monitor the virtual machine at regular intervals. It can detect downed virtual machines and report them to the host.

  - *Backup*: This allows for backing up the virtual machine with resources from the host.

  - *Guest Services*: The guest service allows the Hyper-V administrator to copy files to a running virtual machine without using a network connection. This is the only feature disabled by default.

- The Checkpoints tab, shown in Figure 6-13, lets you configure checkpoints for the virtual machine. Checkpoints are akin to System Restore, in that they allow you to create snapshots of the virtual machine's state for the purpose of returning to a state quickly should something happen to the machine.

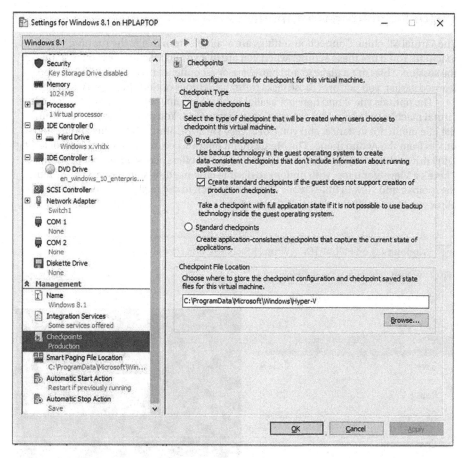

Figure 6-13. *Checkpoints are snapshots of the system state and are stored at the default checkpoint file location, which can be changed*

- The Smart Paging option lets you choose where the paging file for the virtual machine resides. By default it's in Program Data ➤ Microsoft ➤ Windows ➤ Hyper-V.

- The Automatic Start and Automatic Stop options let you state what should happen to the virtual machine when the host is restarted (or started). Options include Nothing, "Automatically start if it was running when the service stopped," and "Always start this virtual machine automatically." You can also specify a startup delay.

Virtual Machine Connection

The Virtual Machine Connection settings are available from inside the running virtual machine. You'll use these settings when you are in a virtual machine session to manage the session. This isn't a place to add hardware or reconfigure memory options; as you learned earlier, you perform those tasks from the Settings options in Hyper-V Manager.

The options you'll find here are available from a menu that runs across the top of the virtual machine window. You can see this in Figure 6-14. You can access Settings from the File menu, for instance, and you can access Turn Off, Shut Down, Checkpoint, and others from the Action menu. The Media menu offers access to available drives, including DVD drives shared on the host. The Clipboard menu offers access to clipboard settings. There's a View menu too, with options to disable enhanced session mode, view or hide the toolbar, and view in full-screen. There's not much to see really, but these options do allow you to work efficiently inside the machine.

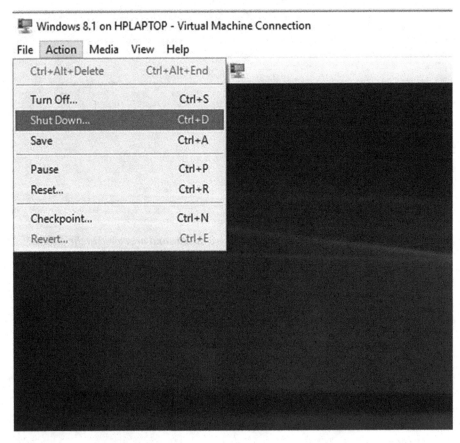

Figure 6-14. *Use the virtual machine's menu to perform session tasks Virtual Machine Connection*

Hyper-V Module for Windows PowerShell

The Hyper-V module for Windows PowerShell offer lots of Hyper-V cmdlets. You can use these cmdlets to automate Hyper-V tasks. The cmdlets are meant to be user-friendly, with commands and parameters created from words that describe the task you'd like to perform. There are too many cmdlets to list here, however, so we've compiled a list that you can use to perform basic tasks to give you an idea of how they work and what's available.

As you read through this list, think about the entries. Cmdlets like Import-VM and Export-VM let you manage the virtual machines (VMs) you create. Mount, Merge, and Move commands also offer insight into how you can work with these disks. New-VM lets you create a virtual machine right inside a PowerShell session and forgo Hyper-V Manager altogether. As you get more adept at these cmdlets, you might find yourself returning here again and again, discovering what else you can do!

Some of the common Hyper-V cmdlets include the following:

- Add-VMDvdDrive: Adds a DVD drive to a virtual machine

- Add-VMDvdDrive: Adds a DVD drive to a virtual machine

- Add-VMNetworkAdapter: Adds a virtual network adapter to a virtual machine

- Checkpoint-VM: Creates a checkpoint of a virtual machine

- Dismount-VHD: Dismounts a virtual hard disk

- Export-VM: Exports a virtual machine to disk

- Get-VMReplication: Gets the replication settings for a virtual machine

- Import-VM: Imports a virtual machine from a file

- Merge-VHD: Merges virtual hard disks

- Mount-VHD: Mounts one or more virtual hard disks

- Move-VM: Moves a virtual machine to a new Hyper-V host

- New-VHD: Creates one or more new virtual hard disks

- New-VM: Creates a new virtual machine

- Remove-VMSwitch: Deletes a virtual switch

- Rename-VM: Renames a virtual machine

- Resize-VHD: Resizes a virtual hard disk

- Restart-VM: Restarts a virtual machine

- Set-VMBios: Configures the BIOS of a generation 1 virtual machine

If you find this interesting and don't have much experience with PowerShell, you can find all the commands on the various Microsoft web sites. A quick Internet search will provide the links you need.

Windows PowerShell Direct

If you need to remotely manage a Windows 10 or Server 2016 virtual machine from a Windows 10 or Server 2016 host, you can do so with PowerShell Direct. This makes it possible for administrators to better automate tasks and more efficiently manage remote virtual machines.

■ **Note**   Windows PowerShell Direct doesn't require either the host or the VM to have a specific network configuration.

One way to initiate a PowerShell Direct session (after opening PowerShell with administrative privileges) is to type **Enter-PSSession -VMName <VMName> or Enter-PSSession -VMGUID <VMGUID>**. Then, type commands as desired. When you're finished, type **Exit-PSSession.**

Another way is to use the Invoke-Command cmdlet. This runs a set of commands on the virtual machine. Here is an example of how you can use this command where VM2 is the virtual machine name and VMTask.ps1 is the script to run. The script is located on the C: drive.

```
Invoke-Command -VMName VM2   -FilePath C:\script\VMTask.ps1
```

If this sounds like something you'd like to do, give it a try. Start with the PowerShell Direct session option by invoking the Enter-PSSession command with the desired parameters. That's likely the easier choice. Then, type a few commands to run on the remote machine.

Troubleshooting Hyper-V Connections

On occasion, you'll be called on to troubleshoot Hyper-V connections. As with any networked resource (even if it's virtual), there are physical issues that arise. Host computers and accompanying servers can be powered off, routers can restart or stop working, physical adapters can malfunction, and cables can get crimped. Before you get too far into troubleshooting, make sure you have checked out the most common problems that occur within the "regular" network, especially complications with the host. Although you'd likely know of these types of problems because of some other issue that's more obvious (like a subnet or network outage), it never hurts to check.

If you believe the problem lies inside the virtual machine, you can verify that the virtual machine's TCP/IP stack is functioning properly using familiar commands including ping and ipconfig, outlined earlier in this book. If problems arise with one VM being unable to connect to another (if they were configured that way to begin with), you can use these tools there too. Figure 6-15 shows a VM running on a Windows 10 Enterprise computer, and inside the VM is a command prompt and the results of ipconfig.

Figure 6-15. *Use TCP/IP commands to troubleshoot a VM*

Enable Enhanced Session Mode

Once you rule out physical issues and problems with the virtual machine's adapter, the next step in solving many Hyper-V connection problems involves making sure that enhanced session mode is enabled and that it's available to the user.

To verify enhanced session mode is enabled on the virtual machine (or to enable it), follow these steps:

1. On the computer that hosts the virtual machines, open Hyper-V Manager.

2. Click Hyper-V Settings.

3. Click Enhanced Session Mode Policy.

4. Verify Allow Enhanced Session Mode has a check by it. If it doesn't, select it.

5. Click OK.

To verify that enhanced session mode is enabled for the user, follow these steps:

1. Repeat the previous steps 1 to 3.

2. Under User, click Enhanced Session Mode.

3. Verify Use Enhanced Session Mode has a check by it. If it doesn't, select it.

4. Click OK.

Locate Missing Local Resources

If the problem with your virtual machine is that you can't access a specific local resource, you need to verify the user has permission to access it from the connection dialog box. This is the box that appears after you opt to connect to a VM from Hyper-V Manager. A resource could be something physical like a printer or virtual like the clipboard. Other options include smart cards, physical or virtual drives, and plug-and-play devices.

Common complaints that can be resolved with this technique include the user complaining that they cannot do the following:

- Copy and paste files between machines and hosts

- Sign in to the VM with a smart card

- Print to a local printer

- Access the host's USB ports

- Troubleshoot a VM without a network connection

To troubleshoot access to local resources and to also resolve problems listed earlier, follow these steps:

1. On the host, open Hyper-V Manager.

2. Right-click the VM to troubleshoot and click Connect.

3. In the Connect To dialog box, click Show Options.

4. Click the Local Resources tab. See Figure 6-16.

5. If you want the user to have access to printers and the clipboard, place a check beside those entries.

6. Click More.

7. Place a check in any resource listed here and click OK.

8. If an option is available to save the settings for the virtual machine, select it.

9. Click Connect.

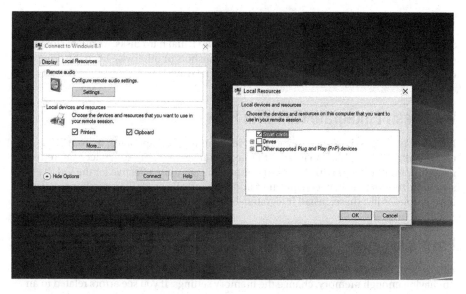

Figure 6-16. *Give access to local resources in the "Connect to" dialog box*

More Troubleshooting Tips

There are lots of other, less common ways VMs can cease to function or stop communicating with the user or the host. These are more difficult to resolve because of their uniqueness. In such cases, you need to pinpoint the problem first and then search for the appropriate resolution. We've compiled a random list of not-so-common problems, which are listed in no particular order, that you can peruse if you are at a loss.

Switches

Connection problems can occur if the administrator created the wrong type of switch for the virtual machine. Remember, there are three types: internal, external, and private. Each offers a specific type of connectivity as outlined earlier in this chapter. If you are having trouble connecting to the Internet from a VM, for instance, you'll need to verify that the VM is configured with an external switch. An internal switch won't work. As far as not-so-common problems go, this one happens more often than most.

VM Doesn't Start

There are many reasons why a VM won't start, but if it's a new VM, it's generally that the host's hypervisor isn't running. The host must meet specific hardware requirements, which were outlined earlier. If your computer meets these requirements but the VM still won't start, enter the BIOS and enable virtualization and DEP.

VM Pauses Randomly

Sometimes VMs pause or stop working because the virtual hard disks are out of storage space. This can happen if you've saved several snapshots or otherwise filled the drive with data. You'll need to create some space on that virtual drive.

VM Doesn't Integrate Well with Host

If you see problems with mice, keyboards, video, network components, or even SCSI controllers, you likely have an issue with Integration Services. These services can replace generic operating system driver files with those that are more effective for the VM. It also synchronizes the time between the guest and host and allows for file interchanges. If you have problems like these, install Integration Services.

Error Messages

Finally, if you see error messages, read them carefully. If they have to do with the VM not having enough memory, change the memory settings. If you see errors related to an unsupported operating system, heed the warning to install a compatible one. If you get an error code, look it up on Microsoft's web sites. Chances are you'll find an answer there.

Introducing Windows Azure

In this book, we've been discussing networks and network hardware, sometimes with the premise that the hardware is on-site, physically available, or remotely manageable, but also making sure to note that computing can be cloud based as well. It's possible to have a hybrid environment where both on-site and cloud-based computing models exist within the same company. Relating this to what we've been talking about in this chapter, a company may host some VMs on local servers while others are hosted in the cloud by a third party. Cloud-based technologies like this are referred to as *cloud computing*.

Technically, cloud computing offers the delivery of network and computer services, including the hardware and software you have on-site like servers, databases, applications, and more, over the Internet. Cloud computing providers offer these services and charge you based on how many services you use and at what rate.

One popular service that is facilitating this change is Microsoft Azure. Azure is a growing assortment of integrated cloud services that is available to companies and hosted via a global network of datacenters. Azure supports almost all operating systems, programming languages, database programs, and hardware devices. There are tools and professionals to help with applications development and management, security, and data administration.

Azure also offers hybrid solutions to help companies make the move to the cloud. Applications can be used on-site or from the cloud, and backups can be performed in both places as well. Azure offers disaster recovery, cloud migration tools, data warehouses, and high-performance computing too. It's ever-changing as well. Each day that passes brings more and more innovation. If you haven't started looking into Azure yet, we highly suggest you do.

■ **Note** With regard to this chapter and virtual machines, Azure lets you create virtual machines in seconds, and they are on-demand and scalable. You need to pay only for what you use.

Summary

Virtual machines make it possible for enterprises to get more bang for their buck. A single, powerful server can host multiple virtual machines. This helps reduce the physical space needed for computer hardware and reduces the costs associated with it. Virtual machines are fairly easy to create too, provided you know the nuances of the configuration options. We covered those in this chapter along with some troubleshooting tips.

Finally, as noted at the end of this chapter, Microsoft Azure can help you move from on-site to the cloud, and you can take your virtual machines with you. We believe the future is here and encourage you to continue your studies there.

■ ■ ■

CHAPTER 7

Troubleshooting Mobile Worker and BYOD Networking Problems

Despite the best efforts of IT staff, it's now commonplace for workers to use their own laptops and tablets at work. Indeed, some companies and organizations actively encourage this practice to reduce overall costs. We know, it's depressing, isn't it?

The potential upside to this, however, is that there's a reasonable chance that "Mr. or Mrs. On Your Case the Whole Time" might be working from home or from the coffee shop around the corner where they like to deprive other patrons of a table.

Of course, this presents its own challenges to support staff. Unless said coffee shop happens to be on the ground floor of your building, you can't pop over to the desk of the person who needs help. It also means that rather than being connected to the company network over a nice, stable, reliable, and secure Ethernet line, they're forced to use a Wi-Fi connection that's horribly insecure, as in the case of the aforementioned coffee shop, or they're at home sharing a connection that's being monopolized by a teenager on an Xbox.

So, how do you support mobile workers or workers in satellite offices, especially when it comes to network issues?

Helping the Worker Help Themselves

This, of course, is the big challenge. Normally if a user has a problem, you'd tunnel into it through Remote Desktop or some remote-control software, which you'll look at later in this chapter. The sensible place to begin, though, is with what happens when the user doesn't have a network connection and can't get online at all.

Throughout this book we've shown you all the technical ways in which you can repair network connections and get detailed diagnostic information about what's going on. Let's face it, normal people can't do any of that stuff. They can normally only just download something from an app store, so you have to use different tools and techniques to help them out when you can't get to where they are.

© Mike Halsey and Joli Ballew 2017
M. Halsey and J. Ballew, *Windows Networking Troubleshooting*,
https://doi.org/10.1007/978-1-4842-3222-4_7

McGyvering the Situation

We don't know if you're old enough to remember, but back in the mid-1980s there was an action show on TV starring Richard Dean Anderson called *McGyver*. He played an ex-spy who would solve problems by creating something like a complex explosive out of a piece of string, a pair of trousers, and a cow. There was also a more recent remake, but the less said about that, the better.

Now we're not suggesting that you ask the person with the network problem what they're wearing...that could go wrong for you. However, asking what else is around or might be available can be a good start.

Do they have a smartphone, for instance? If so, does their cellular contract support tethering? If it does, you might have a usable Internet connection for their laptop. You probably won't be able to use it to get Remote Desktop access, but it at least means the user can send you stuff.

If they don't have tethering or if the Wi-Fi on the laptop isn't working, is there a friendly person with a laptop nearby who might be prepared to e-mail you a file? Also, does the user or somebody else nearby have a USB flash drive so you can transfer a file to said laptop?

All of these methods can help you McGyver a situation to your advantage, meaning you can help the user far more quickly and effectively, while also making yourself look like the hero who's saving the day.

The Problem Steps Recorder

The Problem Steps Recorder was included with the beta release of Windows 7 and was only intended to be used for that and nothing else. It proved so popular with beta-testers that Microsoft decided to keep it in the final release, and it eventually made its way to Windows 8.1 and Windows 10.

You can find the Problem Steps Recorder by searching in the Start menu for *PSR*, where it will be listed as "Steps Recorder." In short, this is a tool that has only three buttons and that enables a user to record annotated screenshots of what they see and do on the PC; these screenshots are then compiled into a single file they can e-mail to you.

Figure 7-1 shows what the user sees when they start the Problem Steps Recorder. There are three buttons (four if you include Help), called Start Record, Stop Record, and Add Comment.

Figure 7-1. *The Problem Steps Recorder toolbar*

When the user clicks Start Record, they're not recording a video, so they don't need to rush with what they're doing. This means you can ask them to click specific things and open specific information and status panels if you need.

When the user clicks the Stop Record button, a file will be displayed showing annotated screenshots of everything they've done on the PC and everything they've clicked, as shown in Figure 7-2.

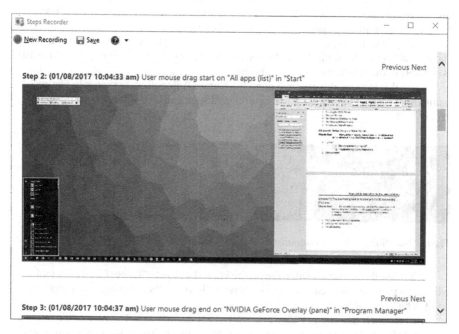

Figure 7-2. *A file is displayed when the user stops the recording*

Below these screenshots is an Additional Details section containing more technical information about the events that unfolded, such as the names of apps or services the user ran.

Additionally, at any time throughout the recording, the user can click the Add Comment button at which point their screen will freeze, and a dialog box will appear in which they can type a message, perhaps about what they're doing or what they expected to happen at that time. This comment will be annotated to the screenshot taken at that moment so that you can read it.

The user needs to click the Save button at the top left of this window to save the file to their PC; the desktop is the default save location for this tool. That file, which is only small in size, can then be sent to yourself for review.

Overall, the Problem Steps Recorder is an excellent tool that shouldn't be underestimated because it allows you to see exactly what the user is doing...or at least what they're doing wrong again!

Game DVR

We want to mention a gaming feature that's exclusive to Windows 10, as there are a few occasions where it might be useful as a support tool. It is limited in functionality, though, and there are rules you need to follow to get it to work effectively. You won't find Game DVR in the Enterprise editions of Windows 10, but it's in Pro.

You open Game DVR on a Windows 10 PC by pressing the Windows Key+G. At first, the user will asked to confirm that the app they're using is in fact a game, as Windows 10 is sensible enough to know what is and is not.

Once this is done, the user can open the Game DVR toolbar, as shown in Figure 7-3, using the Windows Key+G key combination, and start and stop video recording with Win+Alt+R.

Figure 7-3. Game DVR can sometimes help with support

What this does is save a video file on the PC to the /Users/Videos/Captures folder, which can then be e-mailed to a support person. However, there is a big caveat that you need to be aware of first.

This caveat is that Game DVR works only inside a single app. This means it's absolutely fine if the user wants to record a problem they're having with your customer relationship management (CRM) software, but the moment they open the Start menu or switch to another app, it'll stop working.

That said, it's worth mentioning here as you never know when a video of a problem might give you greater insight into what's going on with the PC at the time and what the user is actually doing.

Providing Remote Help and Support

The Problem Steps Recorder and Game DVR are useful tools, but if the user has Internet access, you'll probably want to sign into their PC remotely and take control. Now you might have a third-party tool you like to use, such as Team Viewer, but there are actually no fewer than *three* ways you can achieve the same thing with Windows itself.

Configuring a PC for Remote Connections

Before you can help a user remotely, their PC needs to be configured to permit remote connections. You do this from the System Properties panel; open the Control Panel, click System, and then click Remote Settings in to the top-left corner of the windows. You can also search for *sysdm.cpl* in the Start menu.

The Remote tab of the System Properties Dialog contains the settings you need, as shown in Figure 7-4. Here you can allow (or deny) Remote Assistance (and Quick Assist) connections and also allow or deny Remote Desktop connections. Note that with Remote Desktop, which we'll look at shortly, you normally need the username and password of a specific user on the PC. However, you can also click the Select Users button to add IT support staff from the company domain.

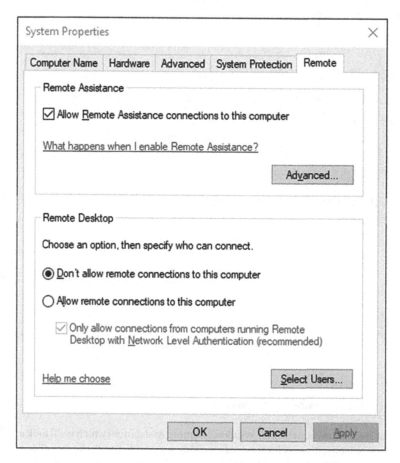

Figure 7-4. *You configure Remote Assist in the System Properties Dialog*

Quick Assist

Quick Assist is a feature exclusive to Windows 10, so it can't be used to provide assistance to or from a Windows 7 or Windows 8.1 PC. You need to be signed into the PC with a Microsoft Account or Azure Active Directory account for it to work, but it provides a six-digit code that enables Microsoft's Remote Desktop peer-to-peer system to provide remote access to a PC, as shown in Figure 7-5.

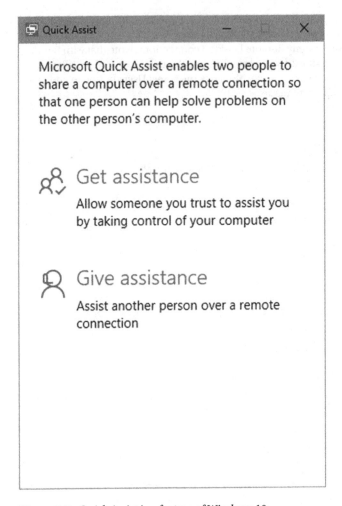

Figure 7-5. *Quick Assist is a feature of Windows 10*

Quick Assist is an improvement over Windows Remote Assistance (which we'll look a shortly) for several reasons: it's easy for the user receiving support to use it, the tool allows you to restart the remote PC while keeping the support session active, and the person providing support can also respond to User Account Control requests.

Along the top of the Quick Assist window when you're providing support is a toolbar containing some useful utilities, as shown in Figure 7-6.

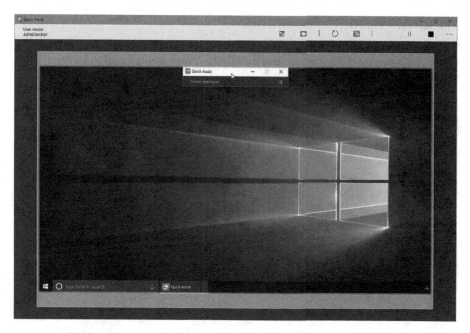

Figure 7-6. Microsoft Quick Assist in action

- *Annotate* allows you draw and scrawl on the screen of the user being supported. You can do this to highlight things for them so they can see what they've done wrong or where the option is that they can't find.

- *Fit Screen* allows you to see their screen at either its native resolution or one that will fit inside the window you have open on your own screen.

- *Restart* restarts the remote PC while keeping the Quick Assist session active.

- *Task Manager* opens Task Manager on the Remote PC.

- *Reconnect* enables you to reconnect to a remote PC where the connection has dropped.

- *Pause* allows you to pause the connection, temporarily giving the end user control again.

- *Stop* closes the Quick Assist connection.

Windows Remote Assistance

Windows Remote Assistance can be found in all supported versions of the operating system. It's a remote-control application for PCs that's most easily found in the Start menu by searching for *msra.exe*.

Just as with Quick Assist, you can either ask for help or offer it, and there are several different options for sending the invitation file Remote Assistance creates, as shown in Figure 7-7.

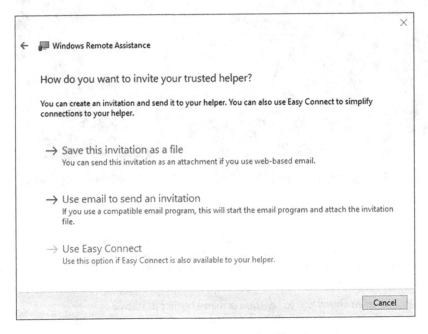

Figure 7-7. *Remote Assistance requires an invitation file to be sent*

You can either save the invitation file or send it via e-mail. This second option will not be available to you if you don't have an e-mail app, such as Microsoft Outlook, already installed and configured on the PC. That's where saving the file comes in, as it can then be attached to e-mail in a browser.

Activating Easy Connect in the Enterprise

Easy Connect may or may not work for you as it requires the Peer Name Resolution Protocol and IPv6 connectivity to work, and not all routers support the Peer Name Resolution Protocol. You will also find that in Enterprise environments this might be disabled. It will need to be installed on the server, and it will need to be enabled on the remote PC.

You do this in the Group Policy Editor (search for *gpedit.msc* in the Start menu); navigate to Computer Configuration ➤ Administrative Templates ➤ Network ➤ TCPIP Settings ➤ IPv6 Transition and then change the Set Teredo State option to Enabled, as shown in Figure 7-8.

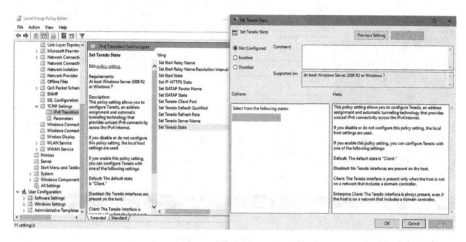

Figure 7-8. *You may need to change a Group Policy setting to get Easy Connect working*

Once the invitation files have been sent, the remote user will need to stay at their PC for a few minutes, as they have a couple of extra things to do. The first is to relay to the person providing support the password they're given, as shown in Figure 7-9. This is best not put in the e-mail with the invitation file for obvious reasons of security.

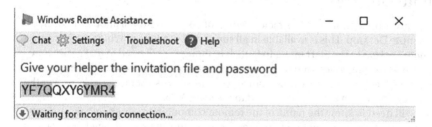

Figure 7-9. *In addition to the invitation file, you will need a password*

When you have opened the invitation file and Remote Assistance is running on your PC, you'll first be asked for the password. Then the remote user will be asked if they want you to see their desktop. They still can't leave, though, as once you have access, you need to click the Request Control button that sits in the top left of the Remote Assistance window.

Once you click this, a message will appear on the remote users' PC saying you would like to take control of their desktop. It is *very* important at this stage that you ask them to also select the box that says "Allow [name] to respond to User Account Control Prompts." Otherwise, the user will have to sit there the whole time and click them for you, as shown in Figure 7-10.

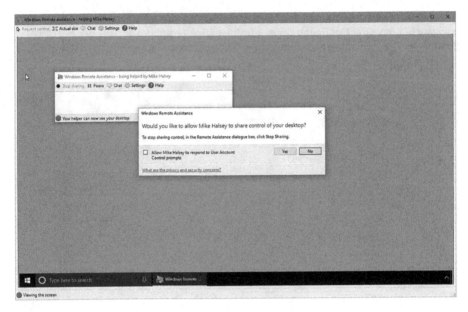

Figure 7-10. You need to request control of the remote PC

Once you have access, it's fairly standard fare from there on. You can open a chat window to talk to the person you are providing support to, and they can end the support session at any time should they want.

Remote Desktop

If you are an IT professional, the de facto method of taking control of another PC is by using Remote Desktop. This is available in all supported versions of Windows. Just search for *Remote Desktop* in the Start menu to launch it, though you'll need to make sure that Remote Desktop connections are permitted on the remote PC, as we detailed earlier in this chapter. Note that in some circumstances you can also use Remote Desktop over the Internet, such as if both PCs are connected to the same VPN.

You will need to know the name of the remote computer on your network, as shown in Figure 7-11. This can be obtained from the System panel in Control Panel, but you can ask someone to type **cmd** to launch a Command Prompt window, where the command hostname will display the full name of the computer.

Figure 7-11. You need to type the name of the remote PC

Once the connection has been made to the remote PC, you will presented with a security certificate, which is just Remote Desktop's way of warning you that the remote PC might be infected with malware or some other nasty thing (see Figure 7-12).

Figure 7-12. A security certificate will need to be accepted

Remote Desktop has plenty of great options available to you. By clicking the "Show options" button in the Remote Assistance sign-in dialog, you can choose the display resolution you want the session to run at, the quality of the connection, what Remote Desktop gateway server to use, and also what resources you want to access from your own PC or the network on the remote PC, as shown in Figure 7-13.

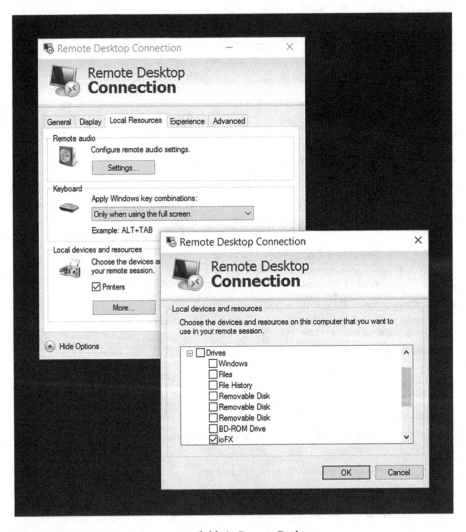

Figure 7-13. Various options are available in Remote Desktop

■ **Caution**   Do not share remote resources or resources on your own PC if you believe the PC you are supporting may be infected with malware.

We've mentioned Remote Desktop gateway servers here, so you might be wondering what they are. They are a feature of Windows Server that allow you to connect to a remote PC over an internal or private network from any Internet-connected PC.

Remote Desktop Gateway (RDG) uses the Remote Desktop Protocol (RDP) over HTTPS to establish an encrypted connection between the two machines, meaning a connection can exist without the need for a virtual private network. RDG needs to be configured for your Windows Server system on Windows Server 2008 R2 and later.

Once a Remote Desktop connection is established, you have full control over the remote PC, including being able to interact with UAC prompts and restart the PC while maintaining the connection, all without the need for user interaction. This makes Remote Desktop useful for those quiet times when the user of the remote PC is away from the machine, though if you're connecting to a laptop or pro tablet, it might be a good idea to ask the user to leave it plugged in so the battery doesn't die on you. Sadly, that's one thing Remote Desktop can't control.

Remote Management of BYOD PCs

It's worth pointing out that if you connect a Windows 8.1 or Windows 10 PC to Microsoft Azure or Active Directory using the options in the Settings app, you can enroll the machine in device management. This setting, found in Accounts under "Access work or school," allows an administrator to remotely administer a PC that belongs to the user, as shown in Figure 7-14.

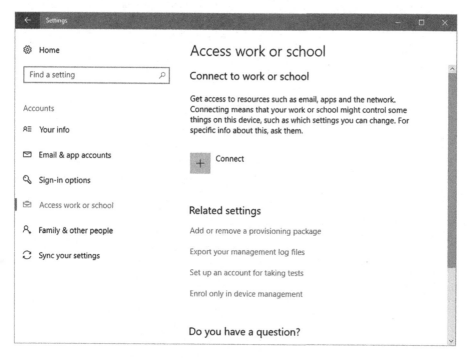

Figure 7-14. *Windows 8.1 and Windows 10 support the remote management of PCs*

This remote administration includes being able to specify that minimum security standards, such as Windows Update and antivirus, are up-to-date before the PC can connect to the company network. You can also remotely wipe corporate data, which is stored separately from the user's own files and documents, at any time.

Summary

Remote users are a pain in the butt, putting it mildly. They might be using their own machine in which case they'll likely be very protective of it, or they might do something that completely takes their Wi-Fi offline the moment they get to the airport.

We like to think that a little emergency pack handed to each user is a good investment; it could contain a USB recovery drive for the PC, which they can also use for file transfer, and a USB Ethernet dongle. This way, if Wi-Fi completely fails on the PC, they might still be able to get network and Internet access on a wired network.

We rely on our network and Internet connections so much these days, but there's just so much that can go wrong, and so many different ways to address and repair issues, that networking problems are still the number-one biggest headache for PC users and system administrators alike. Ideally this book has furnished you with the knowledge and skills necessary to alleviate that headache.

Index

© Mike Halsey and Joli Ballew 2017
M. Halsey and J. Ballew, *Windows Networking Troubleshooting*,
https://doi.org/10.1007/978-1-4842-3222-4

Get the eBook for only $5!

Why limit yourself?

With most of our titles available in both PDF and ePUB format, you can access your content wherever and however you wish—on your PC, phone, tablet, or reader.

Since you've purchased this print book, we are happy to offer you the eBook for just $5.

To learn more, go to http://www.apress.com/companion or contact support@apress.com.

Apress®

Printed in the United States
By Bookmasters